THE BATTLE OF NASHVILLE

✧ THE LOCHLAINN SEABROOK COLLECTION ✧

AMERICAN CIVIL WAR
Abraham Lincoln Was a Liberal, Jefferson Davis Was a Conservative: The Missing Key to
    Understanding the American Civil War
Confederacy 101: Amazing Facts You Never Knew About America's Oldest Political Tradition
Confederate Blood and Treasure: An Interview With Lochlainn Seabrook
Everything You Were Taught About African-Americans and the Civil War is Wrong, Ask a
    Southerner!
Everything You Were Taught About the Civil War is Wrong, Ask a Southerner!
Give This Book to a Yankee! A Southern Guide to the Civil War For Northerners
Lincoln's War: The Real Cause, the Real Winner, the Real Loser
The Great Yankee Coverup: What the North Doesn't Want You to Know About Lincoln's War!
The Ultimate Civil War Quiz Book: How Much Do You Really Know About America's Most
    Misunderstood Conflict?
Women in Gray: A Tribute to the Ladies Who Supported the Southern Confederacy

CONFEDERATE MONUMENTS
Confederate Monuments: Why Every American Should Honor Confederate Soldiers and Their
    Memorials

CONFEDERATE FLAG
Confederate Flag Facts: What Every American Should Know About Dixie's Southern Cross

SECESSION
All We Ask Is To Be Let Alone: The Southern Secession Fact Book

SLAVERY
Everything You Were Taught About American Slavery is Wrong, Ask a Southerner!
Slavery 101: Amazing Facts You Never Knew About America's "Peculiar Institution"

CHILDREN
Honest Jeff and Dishonest Abe: A Southern Children's Guide to the Civil War
Saddle, Sword, and Gun: A Biography of Nathan Bedford Forrest For Teens

NATHAN BEDFORD FORREST
A Rebel Born: A Defense of Nathan Bedford Forrest - Confederate General, American Legend
    (winner of the 2011 Jefferson Davis Historical Gold Medal)
A Rebel Born: The Screenplay (film about N. B. Forrest)
Forrest! 99 Reasons to Love Nathan Bedford Forrest
Give 'Em Hell Boys! The Complete Military Correspondence of Nathan Bedford Forrest
I Rode With Forrest! Confederate Soldiers Who Served With the World's Greatest Cavalry
    Leader
Nathan Bedford Forrest and African-Americans: Yankee Myth, Confederate Fact
Nathan Bedford Forrest and the Battle of Fort Pillow: Yankee Myth, Confederate Fact
Nathan Bedford Forrest and the Ku Klux Klan: Yankee Myth, Confederate Fact
Nathan Bedford Forrest: Southern Hero, American Patriot - Honoring a Confederate Icon and the
    Old South
Saddle, Sword, and Gun: A Biography of Nathan Bedford Forrest For Teens
The God of War: Nathan Bedford Forrest As He Was Seen By His Contemporaries
The Quotable Nathan Bedford Forrest: Selections From the Writings and Speeches of the
    Confederacy's Most Brilliant Cavalryman

QUOTABLE SERIES
The Alexander H. Stephens Reader: Excerpts From the Works of a Confederate Founding Father
The Quotable Alexander H. Stephens: Selections From the Writings and Speeches of the
    Confederacy's First Vice President
The Quotable Jefferson Davis: Selections From the Writings and Speeches of the Confederacy's
    First President
The Quotable Nathan Bedford Forrest: Selections From the Writings and Speeches of the
    Confederacy's Most Brilliant Cavalryman
The Quotable Robert E. Lee: Selections From the Writings and Speeches of the South's Most
    Beloved Civil War General
The Quotable Stonewall Jackson: Selections From the Writings and Speeches of the South's Most
    Famous General
The Unquotable Abraham Lincoln: The President's Quotes They Don't Want You To Know!

CONSTITUTIONAL HISTORY
The Articles of Confederation Explained: A Clause-by-Clause Study of America's First Constitution
The Constitution of the Confederate States of America Explained: A Clause-by-Clause Study of
   the South's Magna Carta

VICTORIAN CONFEDERATE LITERATURE
Rise Up and Call Them Blessed: Victorian Tributes to the Confederate Soldier, 1861-1901
The God of War: Nathan Bedford Forrest As He Was Seen By His Contemporaries
The Old Rebel: Robert E. Lee As He Was Seen By His Contemporaries
Victorian Confederate Poetry: The Southern Cause in Verse, 1861-1901

ABRAHAM LINCOLN
Abraham Lincoln: The Southern View - Demythologizing America's Sixteenth President
Lincolnology: The Real Abraham Lincoln Revealed in His Own Words - A Study of Lincoln's
   Suppressed, Misinterpreted, and Forgotten Writings and Speeches
The Great Impersonator! 99 Reasons to Dislike Abraham Lincoln
The Unholy Crusade: Lincoln's Legacy of Destruction in the American South
The Unquotable Abraham Lincoln: The President's Quotes They Don't Want You To Know!

CIVIL WAR BATTLES
Encyclopedia of the Battle of Franklin - A Comprehensive Guide to the Conflict that Changed the
   Civil War
Nathan Bedford Forrest and the Battle of Fort Pillow: Yankee Myth, Confederate Fact
The Battle of Franklin: Recollections of Confederate and Union Soldiers
The Battle of Nashville: Recollections of Confederate and Union Soldiers
The Battle of Spring Hill: Recollections of Confederate and Union Soldiers

PARANORMAL
Carnton Plantation Ghost Stories: True Tales of the Unexplained from Tennessee's Most Haunted
   Civil War House!
UFOs and Aliens: The Complete Guidebook

FAMILY HISTORIES
The Blakeneys: An Etymological, Ethnological, and Genealogical Study - Uncovering the
   Mysterious Origins of the Blakeney Family and Name
The Caudills: An Etymological, Ethnological, and Genealogical Study - Exploring the Name and
   National Origins of a European-American Family
The McGavocks of Carnton Plantation: A Southern History - Celebrating One of Dixie's Most
   Noble Confederate Families and Their Tennessee Home

MIND, BODY, SPIRIT
Autobiography of a Non-Yogi: A Scientist's Journey From Hinduism to Christianity (Dr. Amitava
   Dasgupta, with Lochlainn Seabrook)
Britannia Rules: Goddess-Worship in Ancient Anglo-Celtic Society - An Academic Look at the
   United Kingdom's Matricentric Spiritual Past
Christ Is All and In All: Rediscovering Your Divine Nature and the Kingdom Within
Christmas Before Christianity: How the Birthday of the "Sun" Became the Birthday of the "Son"
Jesus and the Gospel of Q: Christ's Pre-Christian Teachings As Recorded in the New Testament
Jesus and the Law of Attraction: The Bible Based Guide to Creating Perfect Health, Wealth, and
   Happiness Following Christ's Simple Formula
Seabrook's Bible Dictionary of Traditional and Mystical Christian Doctrines
The Bible and the Law of Attraction: 99 Teachings of Jesus, the Apostles, and the Prophets
The Book of Kelle: An Introduction to Goddess-Worship and the Great Celtic Mother-Goddess
   Kelle, Original Blessed Lady of Ireland
The Goddess Dictionary of Words and Phrases: Introducing a New Core Vocabulary for the
   Women's Spirituality Movement
The Way of Holiness: The Story of Religion and Myth From the Cave Bear Cult to Christianity

WOMEN
Aphrodite's Trade: The Hidden History of Prostitution Unveiled
Princess Diana: Modern Day Moon-Goddess - A Psychoanalytical and Mythological Look at Diana
   Spencer's Life, Marriage, and Death (with Dr. Jane Goldberg)
Women in Gray: A Tribute to the Ladies Who Supported the Southern Confederacy

Five-Star Books & Gifts From the Heart of the American South

SeaRavenPress.com

Warning: SEA RAVEN PRESS BOOKS WILL EXPAND YOUR *MIND!

THE BATTLE OF
NASHVILLE

Recollections of Confederate & Union Soldiers

COLLECTED, EDITED, & ARRANGED, WITH AN INTRODUCTION BY THE
AUTHOR, "THE VOICE OF THE TRADITIONAL SOUTH," COLONEL

LOCHLAINN SEABROOK

JEFFERSON DAVIS HISTORICAL GOLD MEDAL WINNER

**Diligently Researched and Generously
Illustrated for the Elucidation of the Reader**

2018

Sea Raven Press, Nashville, Tennessee, USA

THE BATTLE OF NASHVILLE

Published by
Sea Raven Press, Cassidy Ravensdale, President
PO Box 1484, Spring Hill, Tennessee 37174-1484 USA
SeaRavenPress.com • searavenpress@gmail.com

SEA RAVEN PRESS
SOUTHERN BOOKS, REAL HISTORY!

1st SRP paperback edition, 1st printing, September 2018 • ISBN: 978-1-943737-73-4
1st SRP hardcover edition, 1st printing, September 2018 • ISBN: 978-1-943737-74-1

ISBN: 978-1-943737-73-4 (paperback)
Library of Congress Control Number: 2018958163

The Battle of Nashville: Recollections of Confederate and Union Soldiers, by Lochlainn Seabrook. Includes endnotes, an appendix, and bibliographical references.

Front and back cover design and art, book design, layout, and interior art by Lochlainn Seabrook
All images, graphic design, graphic art, and illustrations copyright © Lochlainn Seabrook
All images selected, placed, manipulated, and/or created by Lochlainn Seabrook
Cover images and design copyright © Lochlainn Seabrook

SEA RAVEN PRESS

Dedication

To my relatives who wore the gray at the Battle of Nashville, Winter 1864.

Victorian rendition of the Battle of Nashville.

Epigraph

After the evacuation of Atlanta, Hood came into Tennessee, reaching Franklin in November, 1864, where one of the bloodiest battles of the war took place. We charged through open fields for a mile under a galling fire until we reached the enemy's works, which were stubbornly held till late in the night, when they retreated. Then came the battle of Nashville, where Hood met his Waterloo.

Confederate veteran Judge W. M. Pollard
(MANEY'S 1ST REGIMENT UNDER GEN. JOHN B. HOOD, C.S.A.)
NASHVILLE, TENN., 1909

Inscription on the Battle of Nashville Monument, Nashville, Tenn. (Photo Lochlainn Seabrook)

CONTENTS

SEA RAVEN PRESS

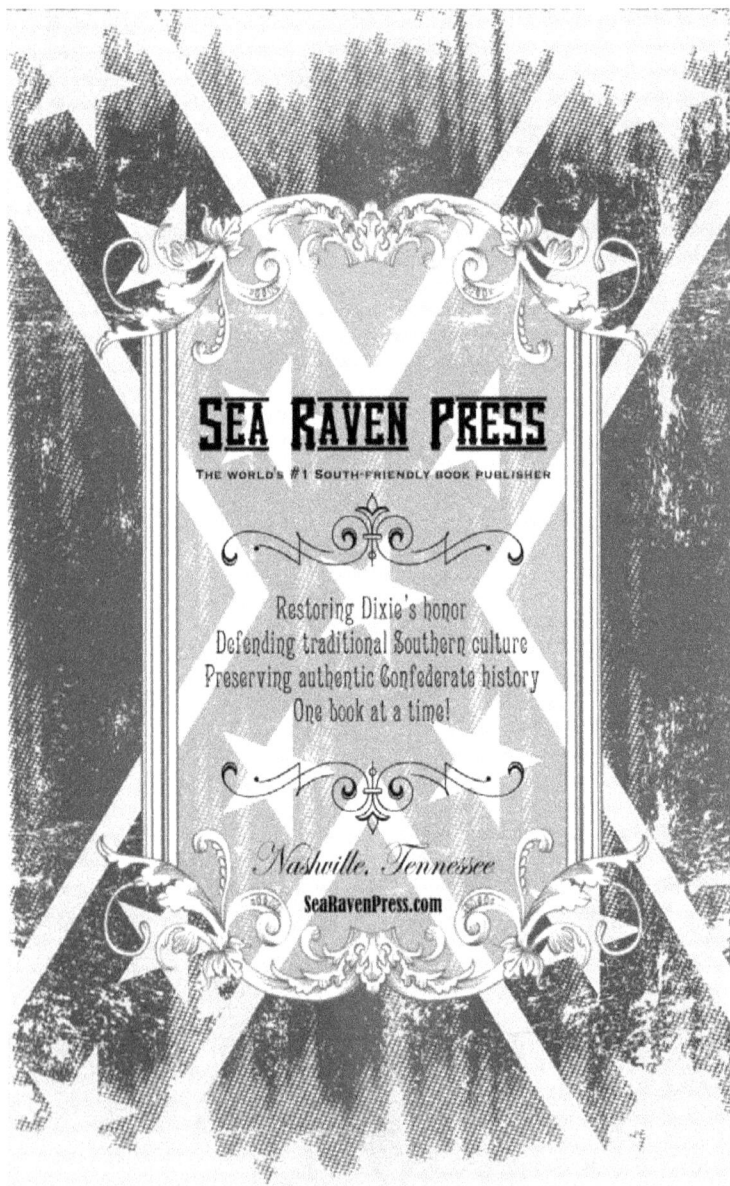

SEA RAVEN PRESS

THE WORLD'S #1 SOUTH-FRIENDLY BOOK PUBLISHER

Restoring Dixie's honor
Defending traditional Southern culture
Preserving authentic Confederate history
One book at a time!

Nashville, Tennessee

SeaRavenPress.com

NOTES TO THE READER

"NOTHING IN THE PAST IS DEAD TO THE MAN WHO WOULD
LEARN HOW THE PRESENT CAME TO BE WHAT IT IS."

WILLIAM STUBBS, VICTORIAN ENGLISH HISTORIAN

THE TWO MAIN POLITICAL PARTIES IN 1860

☛ In any study of America's antebellum, bellum, and postbellum periods, it is vitally important to understand that in 1860 the two major political parties—the Democrats and the newly formed Republicans—were the opposite of what they are today. In other words, the Democrats of the mid 19th Century were Conservatives, akin to the Republican Party of today, while the Republicans of the mid 19th Century were Liberals, akin to the Democratic Party of today.[1]

Thus the Confederacy's Democratic president, Jefferson Davis, was a Conservative (with libertarian leanings); the Union's Republican president, Abraham Lincoln, was a Liberal (with socialistic leanings).[2] This is why, in the mid 1800s, the conservative wing of the Democratic Party was known as "the States' Rights Party."[3]

Hence, the Democrats of the Civil War period referred to themselves as "conservatives," "confederates," "anti-centralists," or "constitutionalists" (the latter because they favored strict adherence to the original Constitution—which tacitly guaranteed states' rights—as created by the Founding Fathers), while the Republicans called themselves "liberals," "nationalists," "centralists," or "consolidationists" (the latter three because they wanted to nationalize the central government and consolidate political power in Washington, D.C.).[4]

The author's cousin, Confederate Vice President and Democrat Alexander H. Stephens: a Southern Conservative.

Since this idea is new to most of my readers, let us further demystify it by viewing it from the perspective of the American Revolutionary War. If Davis and his conservative Southern constituents (the Democrats of 1861) had been alive in 1775, they would have sided with George Washington and the American colonists, who sought to secede from the tyrannical government of Great Britain; if Lincoln and his Liberal Northern constituents (the Republicans of 1861) had been alive at that time, they would have sided with King George III and the English monarchy, who sought to maintain the American colonies as possessions of the British Empire. It is due to this very comparison that Southerners often refer to their secession as the Second Declaration of Independence and the "Civil War" as the Second American Revolutionary War.

Without a basic understanding of these facts, the American "Civil War" will forever remain incomprehensible. For a full discussion of this topic see my book, *Abraham Lincoln Was a Liberal, Jefferson Davis Was a Conservative: The Missing Key to Understanding the American Civil War.*

THE TERM "CIVIL WAR"

☞ As I heartily dislike the phrase "Civil War," its use throughout this book (as well as in my other works) is worthy of explanation.

Our entire modern literary system refers to the conflict of 1861 using the Northern term the "Civil War," whether we in the South like it or not. Of course, this is purposeful, for America's book industry, which determines everything from how books are categorized and designed to how they are marketed and sold, is almost solely controlled by Liberals, socialists, globalists, collectivists, and communists, individuals who will do anything to prevent the truth about Lincoln's War from coming out. An important aspect of this wholesale revisionism of American

The American "Civil War" was not a true civil war as Webster defines it: "A conflict between opposing groups of citizens of the *same* country." It was a fight between two individual countries; or to be more specific, two separate and constitutionally formed confederacies: the U.S.A. and the C.S.A.

history is the use of the phrase "Civil War," which Yankee Liberals thrust into the public forum even as big government Left-winger Lincoln was diabolically tricking the Conservative South into firing the first shot at the Battle of Fort Sumter in April 1861.

The progressives' blatant American "Civil War" coverup continues to this day, one of the more overt results which pertains to how books are coded, indexed, and identified.[5] Thus, as all book searches by readers, libraries, and retail outlets are now performed online, and as all bookstores categorize works from or about this period under the heading "Civil War," honest book publishers and authors who deal with this particular topic have little choice but to use this deceptive term. If I were to refuse to use it, as some of my Southern colleagues have suggested, few people would ever find or read my books.

Confederate General Nathan Bedford Forrest, just one of many Southern officials who referred to the conflict of 1861 as the "Civil War."

Add to this the fact that scarcely any non-Southerners have ever heard of the names we in the South use for the conflict, such as the "War for Southern Independence"—or my personal preference, "Lincoln's War." It only makes sense then to use the term "Civil War" in most commercial situations, distasteful though it is.

We should also bear in mind that while today educated persons, particularly educated Southerners, all share an abhorrence for the phrase "Civil War," it was not always so. Confederates who lived through and even fought in the conflict regularly used the term throughout the 1860s, and even long after. Among them were Confederate generals such as Nathan Bedford Forrest, Richard Taylor, and Joseph E. Johnston, not to mention the Confederacy's vice president, Alexander H. Stephens.

In 1895 Confederate General James Longstreet wrote about his military experiences in a work subtitled, *Memoirs of the Civil War in America*, while in 1903 Confederate General John Brown Gordon entitled his autobiography, *Reminiscences of the Civil War*. Even the Confederacy's highest leader, President Jefferson Davis, used the term "Civil War,"[6] and in one case at least, as late as 1881—the year he wrote his brilliant exposition, *The Rise and Fall of the Confederate Government*.[7] Authors writing for *Confederate Veteran* magazine sometimes used the phrase well into the early 1900s,[8] and in 1898, at the Eighth Annual Meeting and Reunion of the United Confederate Veterans (the forerunner of today's Sons of Confederate Veterans), the following resolution was proposed: that from then on the Great War of 1861 was to be designated "the Civil War Between the States."[9]

A WORD ON EARLY AMERICAN MATERIAL

☛ In order to preserve the authentic historicity of the antebellum, bellum, and postbellum periods, I have retained the original spellings, formatting, and punctuation of the early Americans I quote. These include such items as British-English spellings, long-running paragraphs, obsolete words, and various literary devices peculiar to the time. However, I have corrected misspelled names to prevent confusion, and also *where possible*, inaccurate dates and locations (the inevitable result of old faulty memories). Bracketed words within quotes are my additions and clarifications, while italicized words within quotes are (where indicated) my emphasis.

PRESENTISM

☛ As a historian I view *presentism* (judging the past according to present day mores and customs) as the enemy of authentic history. And this is precisely why the Left employs it in its ongoing war against traditional American, conservative, and Christian values. By looking at history through the lens of modern day beliefs—and, just as heinous, fabricating obviously fake history based on emotion, opinion, and political ideology—they are able to distort, revise, and reshape the past into a false narrative that fits their ideological agenda: the liberalization *and* Northernization of America, the enlargement and further centralization of the national government, and total control of American political, economic, and social power, the same agenda that Lincoln championed.[10]

This book rejects presentism and replaces it with what I call *historicalism*: judging our ancestors based on the values of their own time. To get the most from this work the reader is invited to reject presentism as well. In this

Judging our ancestors by our own standards is unfair, unjust, misleading, and unethical.

way—along with casting aside preconceived notions and the bogus "history" churned out by our left-wing education system—the truth in this work will be most readily ascertained and absorbed; truth that has been rigorously researched and forensically uncovered by myself using the scientific method. As Confederate Colonel Bennett H. Young noted in 1901:

> History is valuable only as it is true. Opinions concerning acts are not history; acts themselves alone are historic.[11]

LEARN MORE

☛ Lincoln's War on the American people and the Constitution can never be fully understood without a thorough knowledge of the South's perspective. As this book is only meant to be a brief introductory guide to these topics, one cannot hope to learn the complete story here. For those who are interested in additional material from Dixie's viewpoint, please see my comprehensive histories listed on pages 2 and 3.

Keep Your Body, Mind, & Spirit Vibrating at Their Highest Level

YOU CAN DO SO BY READING THE BOOKS OF

SEA RAVEN PRESS

There is nothing that will so perfectly keep your body, mind, and spirit in a healthy condition as to think wisely and positively. Hence you should not only read this book, but also the other books that we offer. They will quicken your physical, mental, and spiritual vibrations, enabling you to maintain a position in society as a healthy erudite person.

KEEP YOURSELF WELL-INFORMED!

The well-informed person is always at the head of the procession, while the ignorant, the lazy, and the unthoughtful hang onto the rear. If you are a Spiritual man or woman, do yourself a great favor: read Sea Raven Press books and stay well posted on the Truth. It is almost criminal for one to remain in ignorance while the opportunity to gain knowledge is open to all at a nominal price.

We invite you to visit our Webstore for a wide selection of wholesome, family-friendly, well-researched, educational books for all ages. You will be glad you did!

Five-Star Books & Gifts From the Heart of the American South

SeaRavenPress.com

THE BATTLE OF NASHVILLE MONUMENT

NASHVILLE, TENN.

Commemorating both Confederate & Union Soldiers

(Photo Lochlainn Seabrook)

INTRODUCTION

T his book chronicles the origins, military details, and results of the Battle of Nashville, which took place in Davidson County, Tennessee, December 15-16, 1864. This is not the usual treatment of the subject, however, for here the story is told by its participants rather than those living after the fact, allowing us to procure the most accurate picture possible of what actually took place at the time.

As with all governments, the trajectory of the Southern Confederacy was inextricably linked to its leaders, and few were more influential concerning its successes and failures than John Bell Hood of Kentucky, a West Point graduate who started the War with the high hope of establishing a brilliant military career. Fate, however, had other plans.

Ironically, after losing the use of an arm at Gettysburg and the amputation of a leg at Chickamauga, his real decline began with a promotion. This occurred when General Joseph E. Johnston, thoroughly beloved by his men, was replaced with the lesser known Hood, who was then appointed full general (July 1864), both events which may have alienated Johnston's former troops and undermined Hood's authority. As if this was not enough, during the Atlanta Campaign (Summer-Fall 1864) Hood himself started off on the wrong foot by losing one battle after another to Sherman. Then, strangely, he suddenly charged west for Tennessee, presumably with the goal of destroying Yankee General John M. Schofield and his troops before they could rejoin the main Union army at Nashville. Hood's rash decision, however, left the merciless Sherman free to ride roughshod over an innocent Southern populace, a violent genocidal campaign later misleadingly known to history as "The March to the Sea" (November-December 1864).

Battle of Nashville historical marker, referencing the author's close cousin Confederate Colonel Edmund Winchester Rucker, Nashville, Tenn. (Photo Lochlainn Seabrook)

Though Hood scored a minor victory at the Battle of Columbia (November 24-29, 1864), disaster befell him at both Spring Hill (November 29) and Franklin (November 30), the terrible dual prelude to the Battle of Nashville, where, as we shall see, loss and humiliation were quick to follow, leading to the inexorable and drastic reduction of Confederate power in the Western Theater, and, ultimately, Lee's surrender at Appomattox a few months later.

Tragically, for us in the South at least, all of this was energetically expedited by a fellow Southerner, Virginian-turned-Yankee, George Henry Thomas, who, at the onset of the War, abandoned his state for love of Liberal Lincoln and his left-wing agenda. One of the most infamous scallywags of all time, Union General Thomas achieved military fame as the winning commander at Nashville, but at great cost: his Southern family and relations publicly excoriated him, then disowned him.

In the end the brave, noble, gentlemanly Hood, using outdated weaponry (such as single-shot flintlock muskets from the Mexican War and even earlier) and outmoded military tactics (some dating as far back as the War of 1812), was no match for the more modern methods of the aggressive Thomas (whose men were equipped with repeating rifles and limitless ammunition). Additionally, Hood was handicapped by a combination of inclement weather and financial issues: the Confederate commissary lacked the funds to properly outfit its soldiers for winter operations: most lacked food, tents, hats, jackets, shoes, and even socks. Contemporary writers commented on the blood-stained footprints they saw left behind on the snow and ice as Confederate infantry marched through their villages.

Compare this sad state of affairs with the Union army, which had inexhaustible funds, and, at Nashville specifically, ample food and clothing, as well as four times the manpower and weaponry. It is little wonder the Confederacy lost both this battle *and* the War.

But let us always remember: there was no "Lost Cause" at Nashville, or at any other battle, as our Liberal-slanted history books wrongly claim. The two main political parties were reversed in the 1860s, making the Southern Democrats Conservatives and the Northern Republicans Liberals (the parties would not become the ones we know today until the election of 1896). The Southern Cause (embodied in C.S. President Jefferson Davis) was, in fact, *conservatism*: small government, states' rights, and personal freedom; the Northern Cause (embodied in U.S. President Abraham Lincoln), in stark contrast, was *liberalism*: big government, national dominance, and restricted personal freedom.[12]

Whatever our personal politics, both the Confederate soldiers and the Union soldiers who fought at Nashville must be counted as brave and honorable citizens; men faithful to their individual countries. At the foundation of it, they differed primarily only in their interpretation of the Constitution, the former favoring a strict one, the latter a loose one. The Southern Cause then was a principle. As such, it cannot be defeated or extinguished. Imperishable, it lives on in the hearts and minds of not just Southerners, but freedom-loving patriots everywhere.

This makes the Battle of Nashville a tragic but temporary pause in the Liberal North's ongoing effort to alter, and the Conservative South's ongoing effort to preserve, the original government and Constitution instigated by the Founding Fathers. I am a lifetime member of the latter.

Lochlainn Seabrook
Nashville, Tennessee, USA
September 2018
In Nobis Regnat Christus

BATTLE STATISTICS

NAME: The Battle of Nashville.

PRINCIPAL COMMANDERS: General John Bell Hood, C.S.A.; Major General George H. Thomas, U.S.A.

LOCATION: Nashville, Davidson County, Tennessee.

DATES: December 15-16, 1864.

PREVIOUS BATTLES: Columbia (November 24-29, 1864); Spring Hill (November 29, 1864); Franklin (November 30, 1864).

FORCES AT NASHVILLE: Army of Tennessee, C.S.A.: 20,000 men; 4th Army Corps, 23rd Army Corps, Detachment of the Army of Tennessee, provisional detachment, and cavalry corps, U.S.A.: 82,000 men.

ESTIMATED CASUALTIES: Stats according to C.S.A.: 2,000, C.S.A. Stats according to U.S.A.: 4,463, C.S.A.; 3,057, U.S.A.

RESULTS: Union victory; Confederate power in the Western Theater greatly diminished.

General John Bell Hood (1831-1879), Confederate Commander at the Battle of Nashville.

General George Henry Thomas (1816-1870), Union Commander at the Battle of Nashville.

Loyalty

to the truth of

Confederate history.

U.D.C. MOTTO, 1921

MAPS

Confederate and Union campaigns in Tennessee and Kentucky.

Northern Alabama and Middle Tennessee, the region through which the Confederacy's Tennessee Campaign was waged.

A Confederate map of the Nashville battlefield.

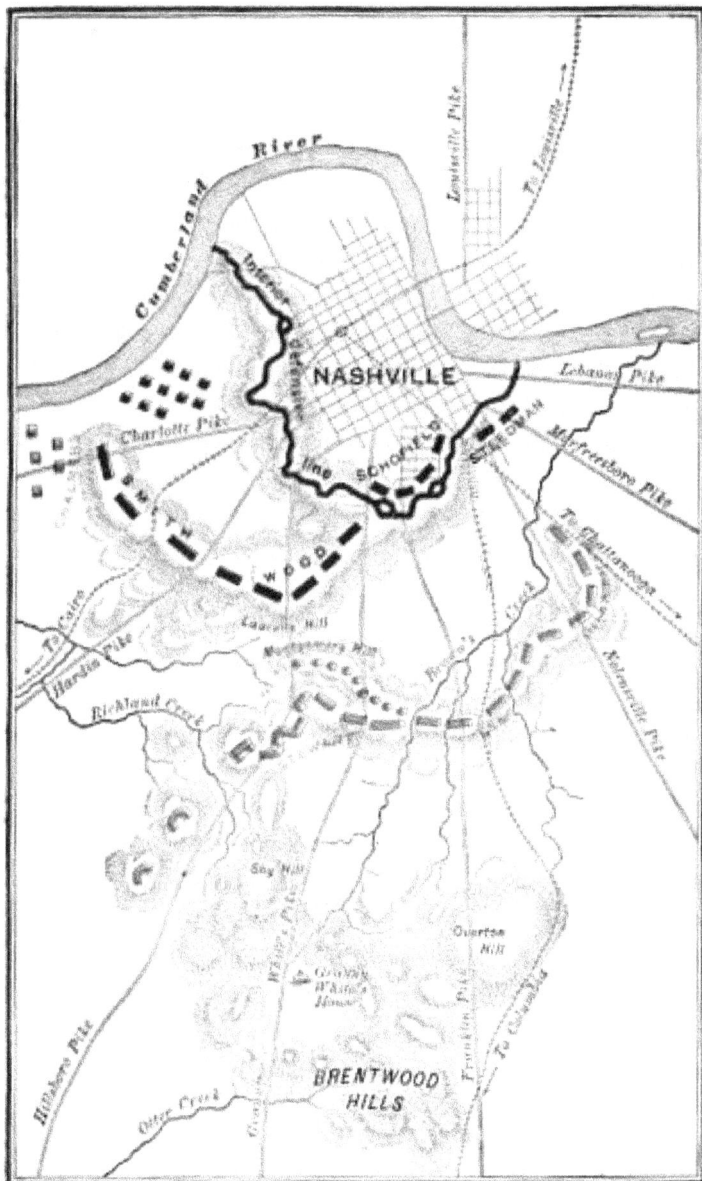

Confederate and Union positions at Nashville, Thursday, December 15, 1864.

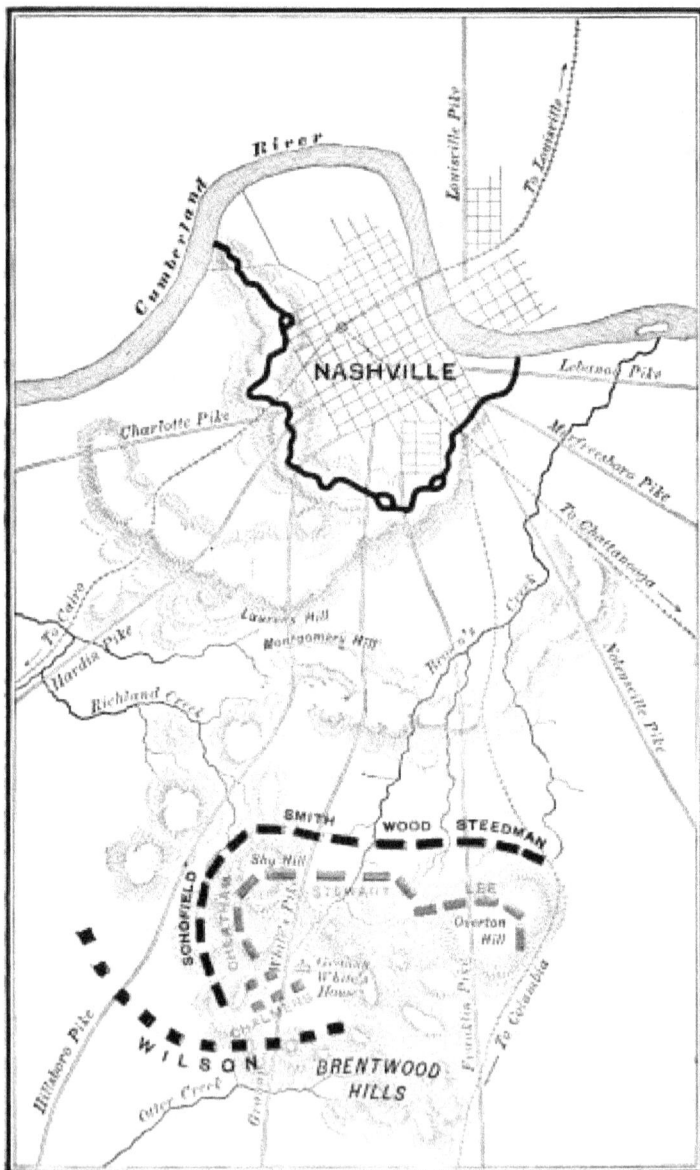

Confederate and Union positions at Nashville, Friday, December 16, 1864.

A Union map of the Nashville battlefield.

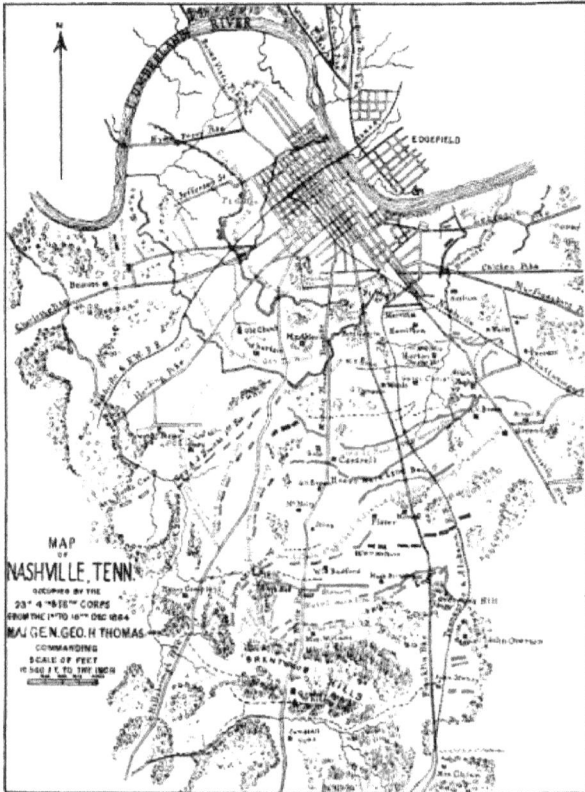

Another Union map of the Nashville battle layout.

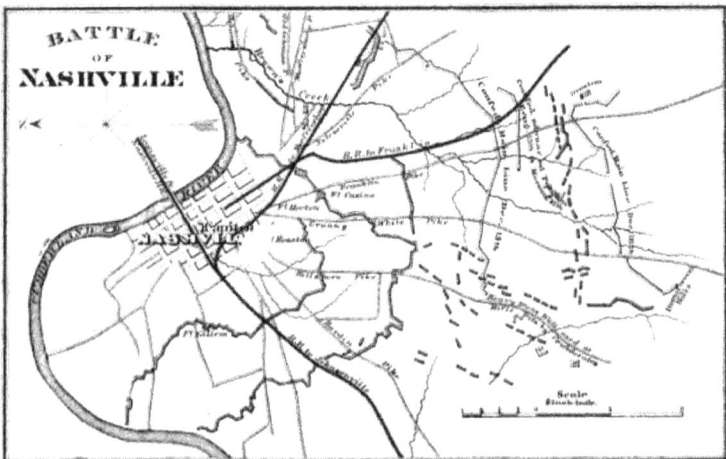

Gen. Hood's map of the Battle of Nashville.

SECTION 1

CONFEDERATE RECOLLECTIONS

Front steps of the State Capitol Building, Nashville, Tenn., with Union cannon covered in the rain, 1864.

Confederate Recollections

HOOD ENTERS MIDDLE TENNESSEE

☛ [In the Fall of 1864, marching] through the beautiful valley of the Tennessee [River] over which [William T.] Sherman had carried his army to reinforce [Ulysses S.] Grant at Chattanooga, our army was appalled at its desolation. Sherman's iron hand had destroyed it—old men, non-combatants, women, children, faithful slaves, were reduced to want. General [John B.] Hood published an order to the troops directing their attention to the ruin of this fair land, and appealing to their manhood to recover the State of Tennessee. The torch, not the sword, had caused this great destitution and made a desert of the valley. In many parts it was unoccupied. The inhabitants, robbed of cattle, horses, mules, and the implements of husbandry destroyed, were fugitives from their own homes without having committed a crime, forced into

John B. Hood, C.S.A.

an "exile without an end, and without an example in story." On the 21st of November General Hood began his march to Nashville; on the 29th crossed Duck river three miles above Columbia, and then, with [Benjamin F.] Cheatham's and [Alexander P.] Stewart's corps and a division of Lee's corps, marched to Spring Hill.[13] — CONFEDERATE OFFICER JAMES DAVIS PORTER (Chief of Staff under Gen. Cheatham)

GENERAL HOOD'S VIEW OF THE BATTLE

☛ After the failure [at the Battles of Spring Hill and Franklin][14] of my cherished plan to crush [John M.] Schofield's Army before it reached its strongly fortified position around Nashville, I remained with an effective force of only twenty-three thousand and fifty-three. I was therefore well aware of our inability to attack the Federals in their new stronghold with any hope of success, although Schofield's troops had abandoned the field at Franklin, leaving their dead and wounded in our possession, and had hastened with considerable alarm into their fortifications—which latter information, in regard to their condition after the battle, I obtained through spies. I knew equally well that in the absence of the prestige of complete victory, I could not venture with my small force to cross the Cumberland river into Kentucky, without first receiving reinforcements from the Trans-Mississippi Department. I felt convinced that the Tennesseans and Kentuckians would not join our forces, since we had failed in the first instance to defeat the Federal Army and capture Nashville. The President

[Jefferson Davis] was still urgent in his instructions relative to the transference of troops to the Army of Tennessee from Texas, and I daily hoped to receive the glad tidings of their safe passage across the Mississippi river.

Thus, unless strengthened by these long-looked for reinforcements, the only remaining chance of success in the campaign, at this juncture, was to take position, entrench around Nashville, and await [George H.] Thomas's attack which, if handsomely repulsed, might afford us an opportunity to follow up our advantage on the spot, and enter the city on the heels of the enemy.

I could not afford to turn southward, unless for the special purpose of forming a junction with the expected reinforcements from Texas, and with the avowed intention to march back again upon Nashville. In truth, our Army was in that condition which rendered it more judicious the men should face a decisive issue rather than retreat—in other words, rather than renounce the honor of their cause, without having made a last and manful effort to lift up the sinking fortunes of the Confederacy.

I therefore determined to move upon Nashville, to entrench, to accept the chances of reinforcements from Texas, and, even at the risk of an attack in the meantime by overwhelming numbers, to adopt the only feasible means of defeating the enemy with my reduced numbers, viz., to await his attack, and, if favored by success, to follow him into his works. I was apprised of each accession to Thomas's Army, but was still unwilling to abandon the ground as long as I saw a shadow of probability of assistance from the Trans-Mississippi Department, or of victory in battle; and, as I have just remarked, the troops would, I believed, return better satisfied even after defeat if, in grasping at the last straw, they felt that a brave and vigorous effort had been made to save the country from disaster [meaning, a Liberal government under Left-wing President Lincoln].[15] Such, at the time, was my opinion, which I have since had no reason to alter.

In accordance with these convictions, I ordered the Army to move forward on the 1st of December in the direction of Nashville; [Stephen Dill] Lee's Corps marched in advance, followed by Stewart's and Cheatham's Corps, and the troops bivouacked that night in the vicinity of Brentwood. On the morning of the 2nd, the march was resumed, and line of battle formed in front of Nashville. Lee's Corps was placed in the centre and across the Franklin pike; Stewart occupied the left, and Cheatham the right—their flanks extending as near the Cumberland as possible, whilst [Nathan B.] Forrest's cavalry filled the gap between them and the river.

General [Lovell H.] Rousseau occupied Murfreesboro, in rear of our right, with about eight thousand men heavily entrenched. General [William B.] Bate's Division, Sears's and Brown's brigades, were ordered, on the 5th, to report at that point to General Forrest, who was instructed to watch closely that detachment of the enemy. The same day, information was received of the capture of one hundred prisoners, two pieces of artillery, twenty wagons and teams by Forrest's cavalry, at Lavergne; of the capture and destruction of three block houses on the Chattanooga Railroad, by Bate's Division; and of the seizure the day previous, by General [James R.] Chalmers, of two transports on the Cumberland river, with three hundred mules on board.

We had in our possession two engines and several cars, which ran as far south as Pulaski. Dispatches were sent to Generals [Pierre G. T.] Beauregard and [Dabney H.] Maury to repair the railroad from Corinth to Decatur, as our trains would be running in a day or two to the latter point. This means of transportation was of great service in furnishing supplies to the Army. Our troops had, when we reached Middle Tennessee, an abundance of provisions, although sorely in need of shoes and clothing.

At this time, I telegraphed the War Department to request that General [John C.] Breckinridge's command, in West Virginia, be sent to me or ordered into Kentucky to create a diversion and lessen the concentration of the Federal Army in my front. General R. E. Lee's necessities were, however, more urgent than my own. The application was, therefore, not granted.

John C. Breckinridge, C.S.A.

On the 7th [of December], intelligence was received, and telegraphed to General Beauregard, that General [Frederick] Steele, with fifteen thousand (15,000) troops, had passed Memphis in the direction of Cairo; also, that Rousseau had made a sally, and driven back our forces at Murfreesboro. The following day General Forrest was instructed to leave the roads open to Lebanon, in the hope of enticing Rousseau out of his stronghold; preparations were at the same time made to capture his detachment of eight thousand, should he venture to reinforce Thomas at Nashville. He remained, however, behind his entrenchments.

General Bate's Division was ordered to return to the Army; Forrest was instructed to direct Palmer's and Mercer's infantry brigades to thoroughly entrench on Stewart's creek, or at Lavergne, according as he might deem more judicious; to constitute, with these troops and his cavalry, a force in observation of the enemy at Murfreesboro, and, lastly, to send a brigade of cavalry to picket the river at Lebanon.

The Federals having been reported to be massing cavalry at Edgefield, Forrest was instructed to meet and drive them back, if they attempted to cross the Cumberland. The same day, the 10th of December, Generals

Stewart and Cheatham were directed to construct detached works in rear of their flanks, which rested near the river, in order to protect these flanks against an effort by the Federals to turn them. Although every possible exertion was made by these officers, the works were not completed when, on the 15th, the Federal Army moved out, and attacked both flanks, whilst the main assault was directed against our left. It was my intention to have made these defences self-sustaining, but time was not allowed, as the enemy attacked on the morning of the 15th. Throughout that day, they were repulsed at all points of the general line with heavy loss, and only succeeded towards evening in capturing the infantry outposts on our left, and with them the small force together with the artillery posted in these unfinished works.

Finding that the main movement of the Federals was directed against our left, the chief engineer was instructed to carefully select a line in prolongation of the left flank; Cheatham's Corps was withdrawn from the right during the night of the 15th, and posted on the left of Stewart—Cheatham's left flank resting near the Brentwood Hills. In this position, the men were ordered to construct breastworks during that same night.

The morning of the 16th found us with Lee's right on Overton Hill. At an early hour the enemy made a general attack along our front, and were again and again repulsed at all points with heavy loss, especially in Lee's front. About 3:30 p.m. the Federals concentrated a number of guns against a portion of our line, which passed over a mound on the left of our centre, and which had been occupied during the night. This point was favorable for massing troops for an assault under cover of artillery. Accordingly the enemy availed himself of the advantage presented, massed a body of men—apparently one division—at the base of this mound, and, under the fire of artillery, which prevented our men from raising their heads above the breastworks, made a sudden and gallant charge up to and over our entrenchments. Our line, thus pierced, gave way; soon thereafter it broke at all points, and I beheld for the first and only time a Confederate Army abandon the field in confusion.

Major General Bate, in his official report, refers to an angle having been formed upon the mound where the line first gave way. If such be the case, the officers in command of the troops at that point were doubtless at fault, as Colonel Prestman, chief engineer, and his assistants, had staked off the line with great care, and I am confident were not guilty of this grave neglect. I was seated upon my horse not far in rear when the breach was effected, and soon discovered that all hope to rally the troops was vain.

I did not, I might say, anticipate a break at that time, as our forces up to that moment had repulsed the Federals at every point, and were waving their colors in defiance, crying out to the enemy, "Come on, come on." Just previous to this fatal occurrence, I had matured the movement for the next morning. The enemy's right flank, by this hour, stood in air some six miles from Nashville, and I had determined to withdraw my entire force during the night, and attack this exposed flank in rear. I could safely have done so, as I still had open a line of retreat.

The day before the rout, the artillery posted in the detached works had been captured; a number of guns in the main line were abandoned at the time of the disaster, for the reason that the horses could not be brought forward in time to remove them. Thus the total number of guns captured amounted to fifty-four.

We had fortunately still remaining a sufficient number of pieces of artillery for the equipment of the Army, since . . . I had taken with me at the outset of the campaign a large reserve of artillery to use against [Union] gunboats. Our losses in killed and wounded in this engagement were comparatively small, as the troops were protected by breastworks.

An incident at the time of the rout was reported to me which I deem worthy of mention. When our troops were in the greatest confusion, a young lady of Tennessee, Miss Mary Bradford [later Mrs. Johns], rushed in their midst regardless of the storm of bullets, and, in the name of God and of our country, implored them to re-form and face the enemy. Her name deserves to been rolled among the heroes of the war, and it is with pride that I bear testimony to her bravery and patriotism.

Order among the troops was in a measure restored at Brentwood, a few miles in rear of the scene of disaster, through the promptness and gallantry of [Henry D.] Clayton's Division, which speedily formed and confronted the enemy, with [Randall L.] Gibson's brigade and McKenzie's battery, of Fenner's battalion, acting as rear guard of the

Mrs. Mary Bradford Johns.

rear guard. General Clayton displayed admirable coolness and courage that afternoon and the next morning in the discharge of his duties. General Gibson, who evinced conspicuous gallantry and ability in the handling of his troops, succeeded, in concert with Clayton, in checking and staying the first and most dangerous shock which always follows immediately after a rout. The result was that even after the Army passed the Big Harpeth, at Franklin, the brigades and divisions were marching in regular order. Captain Cooper, of my staff, had been sent to Murfreesboro to inform General Forrest of our misfortune, and to order him to make the necessary dispositions of his cavalry to cover our retreat.

Although the campaign proved disastrous by reason of the unfortunate affair at Spring Hill,[16] the short duration of daylight at Franklin, and, finally, because of the non-arrival of the expected reinforcements from the Trans-Mississippi Department, it will nevertheless be of interest to note how deeply concerned General Grant became for fear we should finally reach Kentucky. He ordered General Thomas to attack on the 6th of December, and evidently became much worried about our presence in front of Nashville, as he telegraphed to the War Department at Washington, on the 9th, to relieve Thomas on account of his delay in assaulting according to instructions. This order was issued on that date, but was afterwards suspended by Grant.

On the 11th, at 4 p.m., he again telegraphed General Thomas: "If you delay attacking longer, the mortifying spectacle will be witnessed of a rebel Army moving for the Ohio, and you will be forced to act, accepting such weather as you find."

The following dispatch from General Grant to Thomas gives strong evidence that in this campaign we had thrust at the vitals of the enemy: "Washington, December 15th, 1864, 11:30 p.m. — I was just on my way to Nashville, but receiving a dispatch from Van Duzen, detailing your splendid success of to-day, I shall go no further. U. S. Grant, Lieutenant General."

He could not well afford to allow us to reach Kentucky, and finally assail him in rear at Petersburg. Therefore he left his own Army in front of the illustrious Lee to proceed to Nashville and assume direction in person.

At this eventful period General Thomas stood with eighty-two thousand (82,000) effectives to oppose our small Army, which numbered less than twenty thousand (20,000) after deducting the force under Forrest at Murfreesboro.

I had had reason to hope that we would have received large accessions to our ranks in Tennessee. The following letter from Governor Isham G. Harris, written during the retreat, and at the time the Army was approaching the Tennessee river, will indicate to what extent our ranks would have been recruited, had the campaign proved successful: "Tuscumbia, Alabama, December 25th, 1864 — His Excellency, Jefferson Davis, Sir: I arrived here last night, leaving the Army some fifteen miles beyond the Tennessee river, on the Bainbridge route. Our stay in Tennessee was so short, and engagements so constant and pressing that we did not recruit to any considerable extent. If we could have remained there a few weeks longer, we could and would have recruited to a great extent. The men are there, and thousands were making their arrangements to join the Army, but the unfortunate result of the battle of Nashville, and immediate retreat of the Army was very discouraging to our people. I hope, however, to be able to get a great many of these men out, notwithstanding we have left the State. I have been with General Hood from the beginning of this campaign, and beg to say, disastrous as it has ended, I am not able to see anything that General Hood has done that he should not, or neglected anything that he should have done which it was possible to do. Indeed, the more that I have seen and known of him and his policy, the more I have been pleased with him and regret to say that if all had performed their parts as well as he, the results would have been very different. But I will not detain Colonel Johnson, except to say or rather to suggest that if General Hood is to command this Army, he should by all means be permitted to organize the Army according to his own views of the necessities of the case. Very respectfully, Isham G. Harris."

Lieutenant General [Stephen D.] Lee displayed his usual energy and skill in handling his troops on the 17th, whilst protecting the rear of our Army. Unfortunately, in the afternoon he was wounded and forced to leave the field. Major General Carter L. Stevenson then assumed command of Lee's Corps, and ably discharged his duties during the continuance of the retreat to and across the Tennessee river.

Major General [Edward C.] Walthall, one of the most able division commanders in the South, was here ordered to form a rear guard with eight picked brigades together with Forrest's cavalry; the march was then resumed in the direction of Columbia, Stewart's Corps moving in front, followed by those of Cheatham and Stevenson. The Army bivouacked in line of battle near Duck river, on the night of the 18th.

The following day, we crossed the river and proceeded on different roads leading towards Bainbridge on the Tennessee. I entertained but little concern in regard to being further harassed by the enemy. I felt confident that Walthall, supported on his flanks by the gallant Forrest, would prove equal to any emergency which might arise. I therefore continued, although within sound of the guns of the rear guard, to march leisurely, and arrived at Bainbridge, on the 25th of December. A pontoon bridge was constructed as rapidly as the boats arrived, the corps were placed in position covering the roads to the north, and during the 26th and 27th the Army crossed the river. The following day, the march was continued in the direction of Tupelo, at which place Cheatham's Corps, the last in the line of march, went into camp on the 10th of January, 1865.

Edward C. Walthall, C.S.A.

I had telegraphed General Beauregard from Bainbridge to meet me, and, in compliance with my request, he arrived at Army headquarters on the night of the 14th. The day previous, I had sent the following dispatch to the [Confederate] Secretary of War [James Alexander Seddon]: "Headquarters, Tupelo, Mississippi, January 13th, 1865; Honorable J. A. Seddon, Secretary of War, Richmond. — I request to be relieved from the command of this Army. J. B. Hood, General."

On the 15th, after consultation with General Beauregard, a system of furloughing the troops was agreed upon. In reference thereto, I find the following memorandum in General [Francis A.] Shoupe's diary: "A system of furloughing the troops established. See General Order No. 1, 1865, and circular letter to corps commanders, field dispatches, No. 542."

In a dispatch of January 3rd to President Davis, I asked for authority to grant a leave of absence to the Trans-Mississippi troops; and, as the men from Tennessee had stood by their colors notwithstanding the Army had been forced to abandon their State, I deemed it wise, in consideration of their faithful services, to at least grant them a short leave of absence, as well as to others who might be able to go home and return within ten or fifteen days. General Beauregard concurred with me, and the general order above referred to was issued, as the ensuing circular will indicate: [No. 542] "Headquarters, Tupelo, Mississippi, January 16th, 1865; Lieutenant General Stewart, Major General Stevenson, Major General Cheatham. (Copy sent to Colonel Harvie.) — If you have any troops in your command who live sufficiently near the present position of the Army to justify, in your judgment, the granting them ten days' furlough, the same will be done on proper application made at once, provided the men go by organizations under officers, and pledge themselves to return at the expiration of the time. All obtaining such furloughs will be debarred the benefit of General Order No. 1 from Army headquarters. By command of General Hood, A. P. Mason, Lieutenant Colonel, A. A. G."

I regret that I have not this general order in my possession. My recollection is quite clear, however, that it referred in a great measure to the furloughing of the Tennessee troops—about two thousand in number—and of those who lived in the vicinity. It is a source of equal regret to me that I have not the field return of the Army, which was being made upon the 23rd of January, the day I left Tupelo for Richmond. The following letter from Colonel A. P. Mason, assistant adjutant general, written soon thereafter, will establish the approximate strength of the Army after its arrival at Tupelo, on the 10th of January: [Private.] "Richmond, March 10th, 1865; General: In compliance with your request made a few days since in reference to the strength of the Army of Tennessee at the time you left Tupelo, Mississippi, I respectfully submit that, according to my recollection of a 'Field Return' of the Army, which was being made at that time and finished a day or two after your departure, the 'effective total' of the [Confederate] infantry and artillery was about fifteen thousand

(15,000)—perhaps a few hundred less. This return was made after the West Tennessee regiments of Major General Cheatham's Corps had been furloughed, as well as some men furloughed under an order published at Tupelo, and some small organizations also furloughed at Tupelo. I cannot form any estimate of the number of men thus furloughed, because you will remember that all the organization furloughs were given by the corps commanders (your sanction having been previously obtained); consequently the strength of such organizations, at the time they were furloughed, was not furnished the assistant adjutant general's office at Army headquarters. The 'Field Return' above referred to was sent to Colonel Brent, and was in his office in Augusta when I passed there a few weeks since. Most respectfully your obedient servant, A. P. Mason, Lieutenant Colonel, A. A. G."

Under the foregoing order not less than three thousand five hundred (3500) men were furloughed prior to the date upon which the return was made up. Now since Colonel Mason was the adjutant general under whose direction it was made, there can hardly be any question but that the Army, after its arrival at Tupelo, numbered from eighteen thousand (18,000) to nineteen thousand (19,000) effective troops of the infantry and artillery. General D. H. Maury, commanding at that period in Mobile, informs me by letter that about four thousand (4000) of these forces joined him from Tupelo, armed and equipped. General [Joseph E.] Johnston states in his *Narrative* that only about five thousand (5000) reached him in North Carolina, and, adducing the oral statement of two officers, endeavors to create the impression that their arms had been lost, and that this remnant constituted the Army of Tennessee at the time I relinquished its command. Whereas—notwithstanding the outcry against me, and the general declaration through the press that, if Johnston were restored to command, absentees and deserters would return by the thousand and our independence be secured, and although it was understood, before my departure from

Pierre G. T. Beauregard, C.S.A.

Tupelo, that he would be reinstated—nine thousand out of fourteen thousand, who left Tupelo to repair to his standard in North Carolina, deserted, and either went to the woods or to their homes. This affords positive proof that General Beauregard and I judged aright at Gadsden and also at Florence, Alabama, in regard to the Army, when we decided that to turn and follow Sherman would cause such numbers to desert, as to render those who were too proud to quit their colors almost useless.

In accordance with Colonel Mason's letter of March the 10th, there were, including the furloughed men, about eighteen thousand five hundred (18,500) effectives of the infantry and artillery at Tupelo, after my retreat from Nashville; and it will be seen in his return of November 6th, which date was near the time of our advance into Tennessee, that the effective strength of the Army at that period was thirty thousand six hundred (30,600), inclusive of the cavalry.

Thus we find at Tupelo eighteen thousand five hundred (18,500) infantry and artillery, and twenty-three hundred and six (2306) of Forrest's cavalry; to which add ten thousand lost from all causes, and the sum total amounts to thirty thousand eight hundred and six (30,806) effectives, which proves my loss during the Tennessee campaign to have been not in excess of ten thousand (10,000), as I announced in my official report. As previously mentioned, [Joseph] Wheeler's cavalry, reported at ten thousand (10,000), was left in Georgia when I marched into Tennessee, and was replaced by Forrest's cavalry, which accompanied the Army.

Upon General Beauregard's arrival at Tupelo, on the 14th of January, I informed him of my application to be relieved from the command of the Army. As the opposition of our people, excited by the Johnston-Wigfall party, seemingly increased in bitterness, I felt that my services could no longer be of benefit to that Army; having no other aspiration than to promote the interests of my country, I again telegraphed the authorities in Richmond, stating that the campaigns to the Alabama line and into Tennessee were my own conception; that I alone was responsible; that I had striven hard to execute them in such manner as to bring victory to our people, and, at the same time, repeated my desire to be relieved. The President [Davis] finally complied with my request, and I bid farewell to the Army of Tennessee on the 23rd of January, 1865, after having served with it somewhat in excess of eleven months, and having performed my duties to the utmost of my ability.

At the time I assumed command around Atlanta, a number of General Johnston's staff officers remained with me, among whom were Colonels Mason, Falconer and Harvie, Majors Henry and Clare, who, notwithstanding the extraordinary circumstances under which I had superseded their old commanding officer, ably discharged their various duties with zeal and strict fidelity.

After leaving Tupelo, I returned to Virginia and found President Davis still most anxious to procure reinforcements from the Trans-Mississippi Department. He consulted fully with General [R. E.] Lee in regard to this important matter, and, after a sojourn of several weeks in Richmond, during which interval I prepared my official report, I was ordered to Texas with instructions to gather together all the troops willing to follow me from that State, and move at once to the support of General Lee.

Soon after my arrival at Sumpter, South Carolina, I received the painful intelligence of Lee's surrender. Nevertheless, I continued my journey, and about the last of April reached the Mississippi, in the vicinity of Natchez. Here I remained with my staff and escort, using vain endeavors to cross this mighty river, until after the receipt of positive information of General E. Kirby Smith's surrender. During this interim we were several times hotly chased by Federal cavalry through the wood and canebrake.

Finally, on the 31st of May, 1865, I rode into Natchez and proffered my sword to Major General [John W.] Davidson, of the United States Army. He courteously bade me retain it, paroled the officers and men in company with me, and allowed us to proceed without delay to Texas, via New Orleans.[17] — CONFEDERATE GENERAL JOHN BELL HOOD (commander, Army of Tennessee, C.S.A.)

THE CONFEDERATE CAVALRY ON HOOD'S LEFT

☛ [Edmund W.] Rucker's Brigade of Cavalry held the extreme left of the Confederate army in front of Nashville. I was a member of the Fourteenth Tennessee, then commanded by Col. R. White. We were in camp back of the Cockrill place and just north of the Charlotte Pike.

The morning of December 15 dawned bright and clear. Just after breakfast we were called to arms, and, hastily mounting, went off in a gallop. As we rose the hill we were greeted by the sound of artillery over toward our right front, which betokened the opening of the battle. Riding rapidly forward for a few hundred yards, we were dismounted and placed behind a line, of rail stacks on a sort of bluff. The ground in our immediate front was a low level, several hundred yards back to the foot of a range of hills.

"They marched as steadily as on dress parade."

We soon became hotly engaged with the enemy's skirmish line, which lasted for some time. We rested quietly for a little while, when suddenly some one exclaimed: "Look! look! Just look at the Yankees!" Springing up and looking over our rail piles, we beheld a sight which filled us with awe. About half a mile away, but in plain view, there appeared an immense number of the enemy's infantry, as we supposed, coming over the hills and marching with quickstep down the slope toward us, forming into one, two, three, four, five, or six lines of battle—how many, I could not say—and marching as steadily as on dress parade. Their line of march was not directly toward us, but across our front, so that when they got opposite us we were squarely on their right flank and about three hundred yards or less away. In fact, they seemed to have ignored us and to have directed their attack against a line of our troops directly in their front and apparently running nearly at right angles with us. We stood quietly looking on at the masses of the enemy passing our front, feeling helpless. Our line was very thin, and we could not muster over twelve hundred in all, while there must have been as many thousands of them.

About that time the general engagement to our right front seemed to open up, and, after firing a few scattering shots, we walked back, mounted our horses, and rode to the back of the field in our rear. Here we met McDonald's Battalion, led by Capt. Barbour. After conferring awhile, we filed off southward, led by McDonald's Battalion. We did not know what had happened in our front, and never knew until . . . recently. . .; it would appear that the great masses of Federal troops that passed before us that morning were [James H.] Wilson's Cavalry dismounted, and that they were attacking [Matthew D.] Ector's Brigade of Infantry, which was to our right. I think this must be a mistake. They looked like infantry, and I have always believed that they were.

Following the lead of McDonald's Battalion, we came to where Gen. Chalmers's headquarters had been. The Yankee cavalry had run into them but a short while before, but none were then in sight. Turning to the left, we moved eastward up a ravine a little way, then rapidly up and over a rough, steep hill on our left. As we were ascending the hill Gen. Chalmers rode up alongside in a gallop, urging us forward. Reaching the crest of the hill, we were thrown into line, facing northward and down a long, sloping hillside covered with sedge and patches of small trees and bushes. A few hundred yards down the slope we saw a line of mounted Yankee cavalry advancing up our way. Without halting even to form we charged, and much to my surprise they gave way. This was repeated several times, until, being reenforced by heavy lines of dismounted men, they advanced steadily up the hill, and we retired slowly before them southward, until we crossed a small stream and took position behind a high ridge on the southern side, with the Harding Pike just to our left. Here, with our riflemen posted on the crest of this ridge, reenforced by a small battery, we repulsed several charges of cavalry and held our ground until night came to our relief. While the fighting was going on at this point the [Union] gunboats on the Cumberland, though out of sight, threw a number of immense bombs in our direction, which exploded not far in our rear.

About dark the fighting ceased in our front, and we were quietly withdrawn and moved out, with Col. D. C. Kelley at the head of the column, in a southeasterly direction toward the Hillsboro Pike. Striking into a cross-country road, we followed it until we came to a farmhouse.

Col. Kelley had the owner brought out, and he guided us to the Hillsboro Pike, which we reached about midnight, or possibly later, and, turning to the left, followed it for a quarter or half mile toward Nashville. Presently we saw the flickering of a fire several hundred yards in our front, which we approached very slowly; then came the flash of a gun and the whir of a bullet. Halting for a few seconds, Col. Kelley in low tones gave the order to countermarch, and led us back down the pike for a short distance. Some of us were then formed into a skirmish line across the pike, and the balance of the command went back a little way and took position on a low ridge at a

Confederate heroes. From left to right: J.E.B. Stuart, George E. Pickett, John B. Hood, Ambrose P. Hill, William D. Pender.

place where a cross road led off toward the Granny White Pike, and fortified by piling up logs, rails, and brush. In the meantime the enemy had pushed forward their outpost until they came in contact with our skirmish line. They exchanged a few shots with us and then retired. We could tell their whereabouts only by the flash of their guns. We sat on our horses quietly until day dawned, dark and lowering. The mist soon turned to a gentle rain, and later was mingled with snowflakes. It was late in the day before the enemy appeared in our front. For some time our skirmish line only was engaged, but after a while they came on in force, and we were pressed slowly back to our main line. The skirmishing now became spirited, and we were freely shelled by their artillery as we rode up the crest of the hill on which our line was posted.

In a few minutes after we reached our main line the Seventh Alabama came marching afoot from our right front. As soon as they reached us we mounted and moved off hastily in the direction of the Granny White Pike. It was growing dark when we reached the pike. The head of our column turned to the left and we rode up the pike toward Nashville a short distance, and came to a halt at a lane, with a small field on our left. Just then the report of a gun was heard in our front, and a bullet came singing down our line. The front of our column had already been formed squarely across the pike. We were faced to the left; the fence thrown down, we rode inside, dismounted, and were hurriedly marched across the field to the fence on the west side and took position behind it, our line being at right angles with the line of our other men who had formed across the pike to our right. Others formed on our left, and extended probably into the open woods beyond the south fence. Here we became immediately engaged. The enemy's cavalry in overwhelming numbers were already close on our front and flank.

Wilson's whole cavalry corps (as we have since learned), estimated at from seven thousand to ten thousand, was now attacking our small force. Hood's army had been driven from its last position and was now making its way to and down the Franklin Pike, and this cavalry force, including the force we had been fighting over on the Hillsboro Pike—which had doubtless followed us—was now endeavoring to force its way down our road to strike Hood's army on the flank, and we, not over twelve hundred men, stationed across the Granny White Pike and to the westward of it, were the only protection to Hood's army in that direction. We—that is, the private soldiers—did not know all of this then, nor did we know of the fearful odds against which we fought, but we were in fine spirits and sprang to our work with alacrity and enthusiasm. Kneeling or crouching down behind that rail fence, which constituted our only protection, we poured a constant stream of shot out into the night. We could see nothing; the mist and darkness had covered all in front, and we shot blindly out into the dark woods, our whole line from right to left being one continuous blaze of musketry. In all that we were greatly encouraged and animated by Col. Kelley, who gallantly sat his horse and rode up and down behind us, cheering us and calling out to us: "Pour it into them, boys! Pour it into them!"

How long this lasted, I do not know. I thought about thirty minutes, but some say until midnight. It all came to an end very suddenly. While we were in the height of the battle, with no sign of wavering, a young friend of mine, immediately at my right, sprang to his feet and exclaimed, "There they are now!" indicating that he saw the enemy's line but a few feet away. Instantly our whole line rose and began to fall back. Surprised and astonished, I called out, "O no, don't run boys!" but it was of no avail—all were in full retreat, and we could do nothing but make a run for our horses, which were held on the other side of the field near the pike.

What my friend saw I don't know, and whether anybody else saw the situation as he did I cannot tell, but the whole line seemed to give way all at once. And we did not fall back any too soon, for the enemy had almost completely enveloped our left, and in a few minutes more would have been in possession of the pike in our rear and our way of retreat in that direction effectually closed. As it was, quite a number of our men were captured before they could reach their horses. After getting into my saddle with some difficulty, I was hailed by a companion, who had been left afoot. Directing him to climb up on a fence, he succeeded in getting behind me. But all this consumed some minutes of very precious time, and when we rode onto the pike our comrades had all fled, and we were left alone. Going down the pike at a lively pace, we saw, about one hundred feet to our right, a group of mounted men crowding together and cheering as if winding up some sort of a scrap or chase. We could see them but dimly, and at first thought they were some of our men, but, fearing we might be mistaken, rode past. It turned out that this was a party of Yankee cavalry who had just finished up a fight with Gen. Rucker, and had captured him after shooting him from his horse.

Riding down the pike for several hundred yards, we turned off into a little country road that diverged eastward from the pike, and soon found ourselves alone. All was now quiet, and no sound of battle was heard. We went down this road for a mile or two, when we came upon the Franklin Pike, and greatly to our surprise saw our infantry passing down it, seemingly in a very disorganized condition. Just as we reached the pike the clouds parted and the moon came out and flooded the scene with a brilliant light.

My heart sank within me when I came thus upon our routed army, for, strange to say, during all the two days that had just passed we had heard no sound of battle but our own and had very little information as to what was going on over on our right. But now I realized that the battle was lost. After looking sadly upon the scene, my companion and I rode back about fifty yards from the pike, procured some forage for our horses (he having captured a loose horse), wrapped the halters around our arms, laid down in a fence corner, and went to sleep.

Historical marker concerning "Confederate Circle" at the famous and beautiful Mt. Olivet Cemetery, Nashville, Tenn. Many of the men who fought at or perished during the Battle of Nashville (as well as other Tennessee battles) are buried here, including seven Confederate generals. (Photo Lochlainn Seabrook)

When we awoke the sun was up, Hood's army had all passed, and no one was to be seen but an occasional barefooted straggler bivouacking by the roadside. There was not a sound or sign of impending battle; all was as peaceful and quiet as if no war had been. But, realizing that we must be in an exposed position, my companion and I mounted our horses and rode down the pike toward Franklin. Going a mile or more, we came upon Gen. Hood and his staff and a number of soldiers at a place where a road seemed to come in from the direction of the Granny White Pike. Gen. Hood was sitting on his horse very quietly, and was looking up the road as if expecting the appearance of the enemy in that direction. He had a worn and dejected look. A few men had rallied at this point, and I found there a number of my own regiment who, I suppose, had followed another road to this place.

After waiting here for some time, we gathered quite a respectable regiment of cavalry, and under orders from our chief we took a road that led off in a southeasterly direction from the main pike, and followed it until we came to a halt on the wooded hills south of Franklin and east of the Columbia Pike. It must have been as late as seven o'clock when we left Gen. Hood on the Franklin Pike, and nothing had been seen of the enemy up to that time.[18] — CONFEDERATE PRIVATE JOHN JOHNSTON (Memphis, Tenn.)

MORE ON THE CONFEDERATE CAVALRY AT NASHVILLE

☛ The account of the part taken in the battle of Nashville by . . . [the above] correspondent [John Johnston] is more accurate than is generally made by a private in the ranks. For the benefit of the future historian it may be well enough to say that Col. Kelley, by order of Gen. Rucker, was in command of the cavalry, in action, of "Rucker's Brigade." The troop which he speaks of as "McDonald's Battalion" was in reality "Forrest's Old Regiment." McDonald's Battalion had been restored to its old place in the regiment.

David C. Kelley, C.S.A.

The writer is mistaken on the point of being near Gen. Chalmers's headquarters when we made the second fight. We had fought first on Richland Creek. When the second fight was made we were near the Davidson house, on the Charlotte Pike. Chalmers's headquarters were on the Harding Pike. I did not see, or receive an order from, either Gens. Chalmers or Rucker during the day. After night, when the enemy had been repulsed and had been withdrawn from the field, an order came from Gen. Chalmers, through Gen. Rucker, to make good our connection with the left flank of our army. At daylight, without the loss of gun or wagon, we found the left flank of our army on the Hillsboro Pike.

The latter position, which he mentions as on the Granny White Pike, was in conformity to an order to Gen. Chalmers handed me by Gen. Rucker after 4 p.m. The order was to the following effect: "The army is in full retreat. Keep the enemy's cavalry off my rear at all hazards. Hood."

The writer could not give too much credit to the fighting of the eight hundred men left him in Wilson's front that night. Gen. Rucker had taken two guns and selected a position in the rear for fortification, to which at the last possible moment we were to retire. After desperate fighting for an hour or more in the dark and four repulses of the enemy's advance, Col. White, of the Fourteenth Tennessee Cavalry, sent me word that the enemy was passing him on his left. He received in response an order to "mount a squadron and charge any force that attempts to pass your flank." Unfortunately, I was so near the line of my central regiment that the message was overheard. This regiment had, by bad handling, been twice stampeded. I had placed them in the center that I might personally hold them in position.

They had fought nobly that night, but now panicked and broke. The former commanding officer had been relieved; the major in command gallantly aided in the effort to rally them, but, raising the cry that "ammunition is exhausted," they broke for their horses. I moved to the right to bring another regiment to the center. Their break left the Fourteenth unsupported on my left flank, and before we could reoccupy the center the enemy broke through the unoccupied space, separating me from the Fourteenth, struck Gen. Rucker preparing a position in the rear, and left me to throw the remainder of the command between the enemy and our disorderly mess of infantry in retreat on the pike at Brentwood.

Gen. Rucker was wounded, captured, and his arm amputated in Nashville the next day. I covered the retreat on Franklin with less than five hundred men. About nine o'clock the next morning Col. White and the Fourteenth Tennessee Cavalry rejoined me at Franklin.[19] — CONFEDERATE COLONEL REVEREND DAVID CAMPBELL KELLEY

GENERALIZED SOUTHERN DESCRIPTION OF THE BATTLE
☛ The battle of Nashville, which marked the failure of the last aggressive movement of the armies of the Confederacy, was fought a few miles south of this city December 15 and 16, 1864.

Gen. A. P. Stewart wrote to Col. A. P. Mason, assistant adjutant general of the Army of Tennessee: "I deem it proper to say that after the fall of Atlanta the condition of the army and other considerations rendered it necessary, in my judgment, that an offensive campaign should be made in the enemy's rear and on his line of communication. It is not my purpose nor does it pertain to me to explain the reasons which prompted the campaign, but simply to express my concurrence in the views which determined the operations of the army."

For the details of the battle of Nashville contained in this article the *Banner* and the writer are indebted to Gov. James D. Porter, as the people of Tennessee and the South are indebted to him for a lifetime's service in peace and war, as the generations of Tennesseans yet unborn are indebted to him for his volume in the military history of the South devoted to the Tennessee soldier, and the part he took in the great Civil War.

And just one word for the private soldier of Tennessee, the private soldier of the Confederate States of America. No better soldier ever shouldered musket or marched to battle. History tells of no braver man, none with greater powers of endurance, with nerves of iron and sinews of steel, none with more intelligence, none more devoted to duty, and none with a higher conception of Christian manhood. In the aggregate he made the greatest fighting machine the world has known. He often won his battle under the most adverse circumstances. Name any battle in which he participated where his force came anywhere near equaling the enemy in numbers, and you name a Southern victory.

Governor Porter is particularly well fitted to tell the story of the battle of Nashville. As a young man he was a member of the Legislature and "helped take Tennessee out of the Union." He at once enlisted in the army, and remained in the field until the end, first as adjutant general and chief of staff of Cheatham's Division and then as adjutant general of that army corps. He was with Hood in his march into and out of Tennessee, and was an active participant in the battle of Nashville during both the days of the battle.

James D. Porter, C.S.A.

The map [see pages 22-26 in this book] gives a good idea of the fortifications in and around Nashville at the time of the battle and the disposition of the forces in the field. The position of the fortifications and lines of battle and troops during the two days' engagement are copied from a map made by Maj. Wilbur F. Foster, who was chief engineering officer of Gen. A. P. Stewart's Corps, serving before, during, and after the battle of Nashville until the surrender at Greensboro, N.C. The Federals had two permanent lines of breastworks, the inner line running from Fort Negley, their strongest fortification, in a northeasterly direction to the river, and from Fort Negley in the other direction by Fort Casino, on what is now Reservoir Hill, to Fort Morton, and thence in a northwesterly direction, via Fort Gillem, in North Nashville, to the Cumberland River not far from the present Hyde's Ferry bridge. The outer line began at Fort Casino and ran in a southwesterly then westerly and then northwesterly direction to the Cumberland River, a short distance below the present Tennessee Central Railroad bridge. This line included part of Belmont Heights, went beyond Vanderbilt University grounds, and crossed the Harding Pike near the present Acklen Park. Within the inner line, near the intersection of Sixteenth Avenue (Belmont) and Division Street, was Fort Houston, on the present site of Maj. E. C. Lewis's residence and adjacent lots. Besides the permanent lines of fortification, a number of temporary breastworks were built south of the city immediately preceding and during the battle.

Few of the many thousands of people who annually visit Glendale Park realize that this beautiful and peaceful bit of woodland is almost the exact geographical center of the battle of Nashville and that it was raked by shot and shell when the two armies, the one commanded by Gen. J. B. Hood and the other by Gen. G. H. Thomas, met in deadly conflict. General Hood's headquarters during the battle were near the present palatial residence of Mr. Overton Lea, southwest of Glendale Park. Previous to the battle General Hood's headquarters were at Col. John Overton's residence, Travelers' Rest, where his son, Mr. May Overton, now lives.

On the first day of the battle the Confederate lines extended east and west near what is now the northern extremity of the Glendale car line loop. Going east, it crossed the Franklin Pike and passed on near the A. V. Brown residence to Rains Hill, now on the west side of the Nolensville Pike. From there it extended in a northeasterly direction to the N., C. & St. L. Railroad, from which point a thin line of cavalry extended in a northeasterly direction to the Cumberland River.

On the left wing Chalmers's and Rucker's Brigades of Forrest's Cavalry were thrown out in a line of observation extending in a northwesterly direction to the Cumberland River. It will be remembered by his old comrades that General Rucker, who is now a prominent capitalist of Birmingham, Ala., lost his arm and was captured south of the Overton Knobs, on the Granny White Pike, after the battle. Gen. A. P. Stewart commanded the left, Gen. Stephen D. Lee the center, and Gen. B. F. Cheatham the right.

From near the center an advance line was thrown out at an angle with the main line extending to the left in a direction a little north of west across the Granny White Pike and across Belmont Terrace, then the Montgomery homestead, and on across Mr. Walter Stokes's farm to the Hillsboro Pike near where it is now crossed by the Tennessee Central Railroad belt line. For several days before the battle the soldiers in their intrenchments, which were only a few hundred yards from the Federal outer line of works around Nashville, were constantly under fire. The old Montgomery homestead, which occupied the crest of what is now Belmont Terrace and which was right in the line of the Confederate works, was destroyed by Federal shots, and the old overseer's house for the Montgomery homestead, now owned by Smith Criddle, was riddled by shot, the marks of which may still be seen. It was at first intended to make this the main Confederate line of battle on the left; but it was afterwards determined to make the main line, as already described, about half a mile south of the crest of Belmont Terrace. Just before the battle of December 15 the troops in this line were withdrawn to the main line, the original line being held as a skirmish line.

During the fight December 15, the first day of the battle, the left flank of the Confederate army was turned, and General Stewart re-formed his line, now augmented after nightfall by Cheatham's troops, in a position almost parallel to the Hillsboro Pike on the east side of the pike.

The next day, December 16, was the second and main day of the battle. The Confederate army had been formed during the preceding night in line of battle extending east and west from a point in the hills west of the Granny White Pike, extending east across the pike and through the northern edge of the present Overton Lea woods pasture, across the present Van L. Kirkman farm and the Franklin Pike to Overton Hill, a short distance north of the John Overton home. The line crossed the Franklin Pike a few hundred yards north of the present Van Leer Kirkman residence.

On the second day of the battle Cheatham's Corps was the left of the army, General Stewart held the center, and General Lee the right, facing General [James B.] Steedman across the Franklin Pike.[20] It may be seen by reference to the map that the Confederates were faced in front by an unbroken line of foes and that the Federals had effected a lodgment in their rear near the Granny White Pike, so that their only feasible line of retreat was by the Franklin Pike. The advance on and the retreat from Nashville were over the Franklin Pike.

Nathan B. Forrest, C.S.A.

After the battle of Franklin, Gen. William B. Bate and Gen. N. B. Forrest were detached from Hood's army and sent to Murfreesboro with five or six thousand men to take that place if possible and to destroy the Nashville, Chattanooga & St. Louis Railroad, so that reenforcements could not be brought to the Federals over that road. They performed the latter mission with reasonable success, but were unable to take Murfreesboro. General Bate was then ordered to Nashville with his troops, and took part in the second day's fight; but General Forrest and some of the infantry that had been sent to Murfreesboro did not again join Hood's army until Columbia was reached on the retreat [a few days later].

When asked as to the number of men General Hood had at the battle of Nashville, Governor Porter said: "The ordnance officer, who had charge of the ordnance stores, used to tell me we had fifteen thousand infantry in line. Of course we had more troops than that: we had some at Murfreesboro and some on detached service [like Forrest] that did not participate in the action."

"What estimate did he make of the Federal force in and around Nashville at that time?" was asked.

"You know," was the reply, "they had between eighteen thousand and twenty thousand men in line at Franklin, and they were constantly receiving reenforcements. There were five or six thousand troops in Nashville who never went to Franklin. We were in front of Nashville nearly two weeks, and from Rains Hill I could see the reenforcements coming in every day from toward Louisville. I could see them cross the river. Gen. J. H. Wilson had ten thousand cavalry horses. Counting all sorts of men under arms, the Federals had at least seventy-five thousand."

"How many do you estimate they had actually in the fighting?"

"They did not have that many; but they had them in supporting distance, and that is the same thing as having them there. Their fights were made in detachments. For instance, they attacked us on the right. Steedman came out with his division; he was feeling us to see what was there and to see whether he could turn that flank or not, and we beat him very badly."

Describing the first day of the battle, Governor Porter said: "Cheatham's Corps was thrown across the Nolensville Pike, with its center at Rains Hill (it used to be spoken of as Ridley's Hill; we called it Ridley's Hill then, but it belonged to Rains, and we got to calling it Rains Hill). Nixon's cavalry was on our right in open order, running across to the river, and was more in observation than anything else.

"On the 15th of December General Steedman came out with his division (and, by the way, he had with him [William R.] Shafter, who afterwards made such a conspicuous failure in Cuba). General Shafter was commanding a negro regiment. General [Henry C.] Corbin, afterwards commander of the United States army, was there also in command of another regiment of negroes. They came out against us in rather handsome style. I do not suppose they had ever been in action before. We fired but one volley. We knocked down over eight hundred of them, and that was the end of it—they retired. They left in disorder—a bad case of disorder.

"We had no serious action there except with one little brigade. The left of [Patrick R.] Cleburne's Division of Cheatham's Corps rested on the east side of the Nolensville Pike, held by Govan's Brigade. We had but two divisions, and the other—Cheatham's old division—was west of the pike. On Govan's right, east of the pike, was Granberry's Brigade, General Granberry having been killed at Franklin. The brigade occupied what the soldiers called a lunette—a little open work—with three hundred men. They were attacked by the Federals and gave them a bloody repulse, though themselves sustaining a loss of twenty or thirty men, mostly killed and wounded by sharpshooters. The whole line opened on the Federals, and they left in great disorder, and that was the end of the first day's fight on Hood's right. When we made that fight, we were already under orders to go to the left of the line of battle, where General Stewart's left flank had been forced.

"When the enemy turned Stewart's left flank, he had to drop back three-quarters of a mile and make a second formation parallel with and on the east side of the Hillsboro Pike. He was in this formation when we arrived there late in the evening of the 15th. When the fight began, Gen. Stephen D. Lee held the center of the line of battle; but when Cheatham's Corps was moved to the extreme left to support Stewart, Lee's Corps became the right flank of General Hood's army.

"So far as that day's fighting was concerned, Lee's Corps sustained itself all along its line. He beat the enemy and drove them back. In fact, there was but little vigor displayed by the Federals. There was no enterprise, no push, no energy, and Lee, especially Clayton's Division of Lee's Corps, repulsed every assault that was made upon him. Some of Lee's troops were, however, loaned to Stewart to help him on the extreme left, which was all the time supposed to be in jeopardy, and these left the field."

After Stewart made his second formation on the Hillsboro Pike, where he was joined by Cheatham's Corps, there was practically no further fighting on that first day of the battle.

During the night the Confederate lines were withdrawn and re-formed in front of the Overton Knobs, as already pointed out, extending from the hills on the west side of the Granny White Pike, across the pike and through Overton Lea's woods pasture and Van L. Kirkman's farm and across the Franklin Pike to Overton Hill on the extreme right. In this new formation Cheatham's Corps was on the left, Stewart's in the center, and Lee's on the right. Cleburne's old division was the extreme left of Cheatham's Corps and the extreme left of the Confederate line. Next came Cheatham's old division, under command of General Lowry, and then Bate's

The Overton Lea House, one of Hood's headquarters during the Battle of Nashville.

Division of Cheatham's Corps. All of Cheatham's was on the left flank, except Gen. J. H. Smith's Brigade of Cleburne's Division, which General Hood had ordered to support Lee. Walthall, of Stewart's Corps, came next to Bate's Division on the right, Walthall also being west of the Granny White Pike.

On the afternoon of the 16th, when the main battle was fought, the

Federals made a general attack all along the Confederate line. There had been constant fighting but no general attack during the morning. When they made the general attack, they received a bloody repulse from Lee and all along Stewart's line, part of which was protected by a stone fence on the northern boundary of Overton Lea's farm. On the extreme left the Federals bunched a heavy column of cavalry, and there they pushed Govan, on the left of Cleburne's Division, from the field. Speaking of this, Governor Porter said: "There was no panic about it; they overwhelmed him. It was in a little pocket down there. General Cheatham and I were standing together by a big white oak when a ball passed between us, coming from behind. The enemy had gone in there and got behind us. Govan was shot down, the colonel next to him was shot down, and the command devolved on a major. Colonel Field, of the 1st Tennessee, in command of what was formerly Maney's Brigade, but which at that time was known as Carter's Brigade (General Carter had been killed at Franklin), was ordered to retake the position on the extreme left from which Govan had been forced. This he did, being joined immediately by Gist's Brigade, under command of Col. John H. Anderson, of the 8th Tennessee."

Thus it will be seen that the Federals along the whole line were repulsed and the ground lost on the extreme left had been regained. The Federal troops had, however, passed around the left wing of the army and, until Field advanced, regained and held the ground, reenforced by Anderson, were in the rear of Cheatham's Corps. Then a demonstration was made on Bate's Division, which was on the west of the Granny White Pike, joining Walthall of Stewart's Division. Bate's Division gave way on Shy's Hill, and the Federal army poured through the gap thus made, cutting Hood's army in two and isolating Cheatham's Division from the rest of the army. The enemy was in front on both sides and in the rear of Cheatham's troops, and was in the rear of a part of Stewart's Corps. It was then that Cheatham's troops were ordered to break ranks, each man to look out for himself, and this they did successfully, and Cheatham's Corps assembled that night on the Franklin Pike, joining Lee and Stewart, and marched in order to Franklin. Stewart's Corps retired in like manner, as did part of Lee's. This was an absolute necessity, as it was impossible to lead an organized body of men through the Overton hills.

Speaking of the conclusion of the action on the extreme left, which practically ended the battle of Nashville, Governor Porter said: "The enemy, seeing our army cut in two, poured through the gap in the rear of a part of Stewart's Corps and in the rear of Cheatham's Corps. It required very prompt action to save the brigade commanded by Colonel Field, of the 1st Tennessee, and Gist's Brigade, commanded by Colonel Anderson. They held the extreme left of our army; and when about to follow the stampede. Cheatham ordered Colonel Field to resume his position and open fire on the enemy. This was done, causing the enemy to fall back, and then the order was given to retire. This order meant for the men to climb the hills in their rear and reach the Franklin Pike. It was done promptly, but was not attended by anything like a panic. If our retreat had not been forced at that hour, we would have retreated that night, as it was impossible to maintain the position we occupied; and if Grant had been in command of the Federals, our little army would have been captured. *Our army should have been in Georgia lighting Sherman*; but if it was resolved to make a campaign in Tennessee, the fatal delay of a week on the Tennessee River should have been avoided."[21]

Edmund W. Pettus, C.S.A.

The retreat to the Tennessee River was not a rout. It was well conducted, and there was almost constant fighting between the rear guard and General Wilson's cavalry, which conducted a vigorous pursuit almost to the Tennessee River.

"Wilson," said Governor Porter, "had organized a corps of ten thousand, and had right here in Nashville the best-appointed cavalry the Federal army had ever had. In fact, the Federal army never had a cavalry corps that amounted to much until just about that time."

On the evening of the last day of the battle Lee covered the retreat of the army on the Franklin Pike and also the next day to Franklin. An incident of Lee's defense of the army is given by Governor Porter. He said: "Lee told me about the attack that was made on him near Brentwood. Old Pettus was with him there. The Federal cavalry was led by a colonel whose name I have forgotten, an officer of the regular army with [a] white flowing beard. Lee formed a square to receive the charge. The Federal colonel formed his troops in column the width of a company, and the impetus of the charge carried them right through the Confederate square; but they never got back. It is very difficult ordinarily to break a square properly formed, and that one was properly formed by fine soldiers. I have heard Lee and Pettus both tell about it as a magnificent charge and very magnificently led. They were killed, wounded, and disabled in every way."

The weather was bitter cold during the stay at and following the battle of Nashville. Preceding the battle General Cheatham and staff spent the nights at Wesley Greenfield's home, on the Nolensville Pike about a quarter of a mile in the rear of the Confederate lines. The soldiers were half clad and not half shod, thousands being entirely without shoes. When this is considered and the rough, rocky ground over which most of the fighting took place, in many places covered with briers and a thick growth of prickly pear or cactus, some faint conception of the hardships endured by these heroes of the Southland may be formed.

"On the retreat," said Governor Porter, "we had as few desertions as was ever the case with an army under similar circumstances. The presumption would naturally be that most of the desertions would be on the part of Tennesseans, because they were going right by their homes, many in sight of them; but they stayed with the army.

"A private soldier got permission through me to visit his mother. When he got in sight of home and saw the Yankees were there, he turned around, came back, and fell in line. That illustrates how the fellows would do. Barring our real losses in battle, we were as strong when we got to Tupelo as when we crossed the river going into Tennessee. We had practically no desertions.

"*General Thomas and his officers promulgated the idea that after the fight our army was a mob and not under the control of the officers; but there was as good discipline during the retreat as I ever saw. We had with our command the rear of Cheatham's Corps; we skirmished with the enemy nearly all day before reaching Columbia, and our soldiers never behaved better in their lives.*

"At Columbia [Tenn., on or around December 18] General Hood put Forrest in command of the rear guard and ordered Walthall to select an infantry command to support him, and he selected two brigades from his own division, two from Cheatham's, and two or three others. He had fifteen or sixteen hundred men. These troops had fierce combats, but no soldiers ever behaved better than they. They had battles on a small scale, they punished the enemy, captured prisoners and captured artillery.

"We had many barefooted men, and there was ice and snow and sleet."

"We had one of the handsomest little combats the first day out before we reached Columbia. I was there at the action of the artillery. We had four guns with the rear brigade. And I will tell you what we did have too (it was a pitiful sight): we had many barefooted men, and there were ice and snow and sleet. The soldiers would kill a beef [cow], divide the skin, and tie their feet up in the raw hide.

"A little story will illustrate the condition of things. We had reached the hilly country in Giles County, beyond Pulaski. It had snowed and sleeted the day before, and the ground was as slick as glass. We reached a steep hill, and I rode on to its top with the troops. General Cheatham remained at the foot of the hill, and he knew they were going to have terrible times with that train of his approaching with ordnance stores, quartermaster's stores, etc. He sent word to me to pick out a hundred well-shod men and send them to help push the wagons up. I dismounted and gave my horse to the courier. The fellows soon found out that I was after men with shoes on, and they were highly amused. They would laugh and stick up their feet as I approached. Some would have a pretty good shoe on one foot and on the other a piece of rawhide or a part of a shoe made strong with a string made from a strip of rawhide tied around it, some of them would have all rawhide, some were entirely barefooted, and some would have on old shoe tops with the bottoms of their feet on the ground. I got about twenty or twenty-five men out of that entire army corps, and we got the teams up the hill.

"No, we did not use oxen, as Dr. Wyeth says in his life of Forrest, to move the ordnance from Columbia to the river. I did not see an ox during the entire trip. We used horses and mules, and we had enough to do the work, doubling teams with heavy things like pontoons for bridges. We had the worst roads ever seen.

"The skirmishing began immediately after the battle and lasted until we got almost to the Tennessee River."

"Did the [U.S.] negro troops figure in the battle after the attack upon Cheatham on the first day of the battle of Nashville?" was asked.

"No. We saw no negro troops after that, but some of them were with General Steedman when he attacked Lee on the second day of the battle."

The official record shows that December 10, 1864, General Hood had an effective force of 18,342 infantry, 2,306 cavalry, 2,405 artillery, making a total of 23,053. Two brigades of this force were at Murfreesboro during the battle of Nashville. The ordnance officer issued ammunition for 15,000 infantry in line of battle.

Governor Porter furnishes the following list of Tennessee troops as participating in the battle of Nashville:

Cheatham's Corps, Maj. Gen. B. F. Cheatham; James D. Porter, chief of staff and assistant adjutant general.

Field's Brigade, Col. Hume R. Field; 4th (P. A.), 6th, 9th, and 50th Tennessee, Lieut. Col. George W. Pease; 1st and 27th Tennessee, Lieut. Col. John F. House; 8th, 16th, and 28th Tennessee, Col. John H. Anderson.

Strahl's Brigade, Col. Andrew J. Kellar; 4th, 5th, 31st, and 38th Tennessee, Col. L. W. Finley; 19th, 24th, and 41st Tennessee, Capt. D. A. Kennedy.

Gordon's Brigade, Col. William M. Watkins; 11th and 29th Tennessee, Maj. John E. Binns; 12th and 47th Tennessee, Capt. C. N. Wade; 13th, 51st, 52nd, and 154th Tennessee, Maj. J. T. Williams.

Bate's Division, Gen. William B. Bate; 2nd, 10th, 20th, and 37th

Tennessee, Lieut. Col. W. M. Shy.

Cleburne's Division; 35th Tennessee, Col. B. J. Hill, detached.

Lee's Corps, Gen. Stephen D. Lee; Palmer's Brigade, Gen. J. B. Palmer; 3rd and 18th Tennessee, Lieut. Col. William R. Butler; 23rd, 26th, and 45th Tennessee, Col. Anderson Searcy; 32nd Tennessee, Col. John P. McGuire (at Murfreesboro).

Stewart's Corps, Quarles's Brigade, Brig. Gen. George D. Johnston; 42nd, 46th, 49th, 53rd, and 55th Tennessee, Capt. A. M. Duncan; 48th Tennessee, Col. William M. Vorhies.

When the Army of Tennessee reached Tupelo, Miss., from the 5th of January, 1865, to the 12th (the last date was the time of Cheatham's arrival), the effective total of the infantry was 14,870. Deducting this from the effective infantry on the 10th of December, 1864, which was 18,342, the result will show the losses sustained at the battle of Nashville and the combat in front of Murfreesboro, less the absence of the 4th, 5th, 31st, 33rd, 38th, 6th, 9th, 12th, 47th, 73rd, 51st, 52nd, 154th, 46th, and 55th Tennessee Regiments, furloughed at Corinth by Cheatham by command of General Hood. Two thousand

"2,000 covered all Confederate losses at Nashville."

covered all losses at Nashville. This includes killed, wounded, and missing. A large per cent were slightly wounded and never left the ranks, and many of the missing walked across three States and joined their colors in North Carolina and were paroled with their comrades.

General Hood, in his official report, said: "The Tennessee troops entered the State with high hopes as they approached their homes. When the fortunes of war were against us, the same faithful soldiers remained true to their flag, and, with rare exceptions, followed it in retreat as they had borne it in advance."[22] — CONFEDERATE OFFICER JAMES DAVIS PORTER (Chief of Staff under Cheatham, as reported by M. B. Morton, managing editor, *Nashville Banner*)

MY EXPERIENCES AT NASHVILLE

☛ [I was part of] . . . Hood's expedition into Tennessee. The writer had some strenuous experience in that, and was devoutly thankful for escaping the awful slaughter at Franklin, and perhaps more so a little later in the battle at Nashville.

Adams's Brigade of [William Wing] Loring's Division (commanded by Colonel Lowry in the battle of Nashville) occupied the line just to the left of the Franklin Pike and I believe the division covering that thoroughfare. The Federals attacked us about 10 A.M., but we held our own with their three lines of battle all day. Late in the afternoon the extreme left of our army gave way when the enemy began rapidly turning our left flank. To prevent that we were ordered to move by the right flank double quick. A soldier was shot and fell out of the column. Thinking it was a messmate, I ran back some one hundred and fifty yards and found it was Lieutenant Berryhill, of the next company, and that he was dead. Retracing my steps as fast as I could, I found the command rapidly falling back. Just then Lieut. Pat Henry, of General Adams's staff, came along and, taking in the situation, stopped about forty of us and commanded us to "deploy." In a moment the little skirmish line was formed. He then commanded "Forward," and in another minute the line was in the trenches hotly engaging the three long blue lines of the enemy, who were trying hard to pass our *chevaux-de-frise*. We held them long enough to re-form our main line of battle, when we were run over and captured.

We were sent to Camp Douglas, which seemed the worst fate that could befall us. To tell the hardships there would take too much space. . . . I saw the Federal soldier climb the flag mast and adjust the rope that had been misplaced while lowering to half-mast in honor of [the death of] Lincoln, and in coming down I saw him fall ninety feet. I heard a prisoner say: "There goes a messenger to Lincoln."

I thought my hardships there were great, and so they were; but on returning home after the close I found that only a few days after my capture my messmates and bedfellows, Colonel Sykes, Captain Perry, and Will Owen, had all been killed by a tree falling across them while asleep in camp; and had I not been captured, I would doubtless have shared their fate.[23] — CONFEDERATE SOLDIER J. W. COOK (43rd Mississippi Infantry)

CORPS COMMANDER'S REPORT ON THE BATTLE

☛ The bloody battle of Franklin was fought November 30, 1864, ending about midnight. The Union army, under Gen. Schofield, abandoned the field, and retreated toward Nashville during the night, and on arrival took position within the intrenchments surrounding the city, and there they remained till December 15. Gen. Thomas made no aggressive forward movement, but steadily received reënforcements, and by the 15th of December he had about 43,000 infantry and 12,000 cavalry. Livermore says his effective force was 49,772 men.

The Union troops occupied the intrenchments as follows: Gen. Schofield's army (Twenty-Third Corps) was on the Union left, reaching the river (east); Gen. Wood's army (Fourth Corps) in the center, and Gen. [Andrew J.] Smith's army on the right, extending to the river (west); Gen. Wilson's Cavalry Corps in the rear of Gen. Smith's Army Corps, near the river; Gen. Steedman's Division was also intrenched along the river, a little outside of the main line of intrenchments on the east. There was also an inside line of intrenchments occupied by Gen. Donaldson's quartermaster men (armed), guarding the west of the city, when Thomas's army moved out of its intrenchments to give battle.

The Confederate army under Gen. Hood pursued the Union army on the morning of December 1 (after the battle of Franklin), and, arriving in front of Nashville December 2, began intrenching itself about one mile from the Union intrenchments around the city, Cheatham's Corps being on the right and extending across the Nolensville Pike and resting on the railroad from Nashville to Murfreesboro, and extending west almost to the Franklin Pike. Lee's Corps occupied the center, covering the Franklin Pike and extending almost to the Granny White Pike. Stewart's Corps was on the left, covering the Granny White and Hillsboro Pikes, leaving on Hood's left to the river on the west an open space or distance more than equal to the front occupied by his entire army, from the Hillsboro Pike to the river (west), and through which ran the Harding and Charlotte Pikes. This large area was covered by one brigade of cavalry under Gen. Chalmers (about 1,000 strong), and for a little while one brigade of infantry under Gen. Ector on the Harding Pike. Gen. Hood had strengthened his right flank by a redoubt on Rains Hill, near the Nolensville Pike, and some smaller works near the railroad, and his left flank by five redoubts on both sides and to the west of the Hillsboro Pike; also by a strong line of rifle pits on Montgomery Hill, in advance of and on the left front of his main line. Two of these redoubts west of the pike were from a mile to a mile and a half from the left of Gen. Stewart's Corps, and occupied by artillery and small garrisons of from 150 to 200 men. The effective force of Gen. Hood's army was about 23,207 men (Livermore), a difference of 26,565 men in favor of Gen. Thomas's army, and greater than Hood's entire army.

Benjamin F. Cheatham, C.S.A.

These were the relative positions and numbers of the two armies on the evening of December 14 preceding the battle. The weather had been intensely cold, and sleeting from about December 9 to December 14.

Gen. Thomas's plan of battle was admirable. Taking advantage of the unoccupied area on Hood's left flank and between it and the river on the left, after he filled the intrenchments in front of Cheatham's and Lee's Corps with the garrison proper of Nashville and armed quartermaster employees on a short interior line, he then thrust his entire army west of the Hillsboro Pike into this open space, Wilson's 12,000 cavalry leading and brushing Chalmers's small force away, followed by A. J. Smith's army, then next by Wood's army, then by Schofield's army, placing all this force diagonally across Hood's left flank. His "success was due chiefly to a tactical combination of a superior force." The battle began by Gen. Steedman's attacking the extreme right of the Confederate line, and near the railroad (as a diversion), while the great flanking movement of Thomas's entire army was in progress and being developed. This movement was rapidly developed, Thomas's 12,000 cavalry constantly swinging around to the left, followed by the three great armies of Smith, Wood, and Schofield. Soon the cavalry had reached the left and rear of Gen. Stewart's Corps, and got in the rear of the divisions of Walthall, Loring, and French. The advanced rifle pits on Montgomery Hill and the two left redoubts across the Hillsboro Pike were, in succession, overwhelmed and carried, and Stewart's left (the left of Hood's army) was completely turned by the great swinging and encircling movement to the left by Thomas's army. Reenforcements were called from Lee's Corps, and they were sent by brigades until one of his divisions (Johnson's) was sent. Lee's line at first was thin, and after one division was taken out he had only a thin skirmish line, opposed by the well-filled intrenchments of the enemy in his front. The brigades sent by Lee to reënforce Stewart arrived after the redoubts on Stewart's left had been taken, and were rapidly overwhelmed in succession by the great swinging movement, which soon got to the rear of Walthall's and Loring's Divisions, and they had to rapidly fall back toward the Granny White Pike, taking position near dark on the ridges between the Hillsboro and Granny White Pikes. Night is all that prevented Stewart's force being cut off entirely.

The first day's battle, and the complete turning of Hood's left flank, necessitated a new line of battle by Hood, during the night of the 15th and 16th of December. This line was formed about one and one-half or two miles farther south. Cheatham's Corps was moved from the extreme right of Hood's line to the extreme left, and formed near the Brentwood hills, to the left of the Granny White Pike. Stewart's Corps was on his right, and Lee's Corps then became the right of the Confederate army, resting on Overton Hill, on the Franklin Pike. Cheatham's right division, under Gen. Bate, occupied Shy Hill to the left of Granny White Pike, and his line was facing west, with Chalmers's Cavalry on his left, and on both sides of the pike. Stewart's Corps was between the Granny White Pike and the Franklin Pike, and Lee's Corps holding Overton Hill and the space to the left of Franklin Pike to Stewart's right. Hood's line of battle was shorter almost one-half, and better than the one he had abandoned on the night of the 15th of December. Here he awaited the attack of the enemy on December 16. His position was a critical one; it virtually left but one road (the Franklin

Pike) for his army to escape on in case of disaster. Wilson's Cavalry virtually held the Granny White Pike, on Hood's extreme left.

It took some time for Thomas's army to move up and confront Hood's army in its new position, but it gradually did so during the morning of December 16, and his forces were arranged as follows: Gens. Steedman and Wood confronted Lee on the Franklin Pike; Wood and Smith confronted Lee and Stewart between the Franklin and Granny White Pikes; Smith and Schofield at Shy Hill and around Cheatham's Corps, with Wilson's Cavalry Corps on the left of Cheatham, and continuing the turning operations of the day before toward the Franklin Pike, now the only road open for Hood's escape. Gen. Thomas, having virtually cut off Hood's retrograde movement on all pikes except the Franklin Pike, determined to crush Hood's extreme right on Overton Hill, so as to cut off Stewart and Cheatham from the Franklin Pike. Gen. Hood anticipated this movement, and he instructed Lee to hold that pike at all hazards, and in case of disaster Stewart was to hold the Franklin Pike at Brentwood till Lee's Corps had passed to the rear.

While the great flanking movement on Hood's left was being perfected by Thomas on the morning of December 16 for a continuation of development of Hood's left in his new position, he ordered Wood and Steedman to assault Overton Hill (Hood's extreme right). The assault was preceded by a most terrific concentrated fire of artillery for two hours, from 9 to 11 A.M. Then the assault was made on the narrow hill by two brigades of white troops of Wood's Corps and two brigades of negro troops in Steedman's Division. The assault was gallantly made, some of the troops getting within thirty yards of the stone fence occupied by Clayton's Division,

East Broadway area of Nashville as it looks today. The Cumberland River is just beyond the trees on the right. (Photo Lochlainn Seabrook)

and one brigade of Stephenson's Division on Clayton's left (all of Lee's Corps). The assaults were made several times, and so determinedly that one-half of the loss of Thomas's entire army occurred in the attempts to carry Overton Hill and seize the Franklin Pike to cut off Hood's other two corps to Lee's left. The repeated assaults were repulsed with great slaughter, the last assault being repulsed and the enemy retiring out of sight about 3:30 P.M.; and virtually enabling Hood to feel secure on that pike, so far as defeat on that part of his army might occur. So anxious was Hood about his right flank that he sent Cleburne's Old Division from his extreme left to his extreme right to help hold that pike during the repeated assaults. These troops, however, were soon recalled to meet disaster on the left, and were not used by Lee in repulsing the enemy.

About the time of the last repulse of the enemy at Overton Hill (3:30 or 4 P.M.) the great army of Thomas's had again enveloped Hood's left flank, Wilson's Cavalry working over and around Cheatham's left flank, and getting across the Granny White Pike and in rear of the Confederate left flank, as it did the day before. About this time also the angle held by Cheatham's right (Shy Hill), just west of the Granny White Pike, and near Stewart's left flank (the left center of Hood's army), was captured by the Union troops, causing a break almost in the entire Confederate army, and almost a mad rush in panic over the hills toward the Franklin Pike by the Confederate troops to the left of that pike. The enemy rushed into the space of the broken Confederate line, Stewart's and Cheatham's Corps rushed toward the Franklin Pike, and the entire Union army charged and pursued from the direction of the Granny White Pike and toward the rear of Lee's Corps, which also gave way gradually. Clayton's Division, forming a second line between Overton Hill and Brentwood to hold in check the enemy, came from the direction of the Granny White Pike. All that saved Hood's army at this critical moment was the fact that Lee formed this second line and held in check the enemy. Fortunately there was no pursuit by the left of Wood's Corps and Steedman's Division on the Franklin Pike until it was too late to take advantage of the rear movement of Lee's Corps from Overton Hill. While Lee was holding the enemy in check with his rearguard he was notified near dark that the enemy were about reaching Brentwood. He rapidly withdrew, arriving at Brentwood about dark. He found that Stewart and Cheatham had already passed Brentwood, moving to the rear, that Chalmers's Cavalry at dark was fighting Wilson's Cavalry less than half a mile from the Franklin Pike. Lee rapidly passed by Brentwood, followed by Chalmers's Cavalry, halting his rear guard six miles north of Franklin at 10 P.M., sending a small command to hold a gap east of where he halted in the hills.

Lee was ordered by Gen. Hood to cover the retreat of his army from the great defeat at Nashville. The rest of the army, in great confusion and disorder, had moved on to Franklin. Smith's Army Corps and part of Wilson's Cavalry were east of the Granny White Pike at dark, and Wilson's Cavalry less than one-half mile of the Franklin Pike, near Brentwood. Most of Wood's Corps were between the Granny White Pike and the Franklin Pike, and Wood's and Smith's armies pressed from the direction of the Granny White Pike.

The battle of Nashville was the most complete victory of the war, and won by the Union army. The Confederate army, although it held the field at Franklin, was terribly punished and much demoralized by its great losses, but covered itself with a halo of valor equal to any display on any field of the great war on either side. The army realized that Hood's campaign was a forlorn hope, and that the Confederacy was on its last legs; yet the Confederate soldier, true to his duty and in face of inevitable defeat, maintained a bold front, waiting for final order of his government to desist or to be crushed finally.

It is difficult to get at Hood's losses. He claims to have lost 54 guns and 10,000 men, including his loss at Franklin (about 6,252 men killed, wounded, and prisoners). Livermore puts his prisoners at Nashville at 4,462 men, and Thomas's army lost 3,061 men. Hood did not lose many men killed and wounded, as he was really flanked and maneuvered into a rout by Thomas. He could not move his guns, as the horses were in the rear for safety, and the break the second day was so sudden and rapid that the horses could not be brought up.

[Regarding the pursuit,] as stated, Lee, with the rear guard, composed of Clayton's Division (brigades of Gibson, Holtzclaw, and Stovall), passed Brentwood after dark. He was ordered by Gen. Hood to cover the retreat of his army. His first halt was at Hollow Tree Gap, about six miles north of Franklin. Here, with Pettus's Brigade, Stephenson's Division and Stovall's Brigade, Clayton's Division and Bledsoe's Battery, he awaited the enemy. Wilson's Cavalry appeared about 8 A.M., driving Chalmers's Cavalry and actually many of them passing through the infantry rear guard; but they were repulsed with loss of men and

"The battle of Nashville was the most complete victory of the war, and won by the Union army."

guidons. They again appeared at 9 A.M., and were driven back with the loss of one hundred prisoners and several guidons. The retreat was then resumed toward Franklin, and, although frequently attacked, got over the Harpeth River with loss of some prisoners; and the trestle bridge was destroyed.

The next stand was made about one and one-half miles south of Franklin, as that city was full of wounded of both armies from the battle of Franklin [November 30, 1864]. Here the pursuit was again checked, and here it was that Gen. Lee was wounded while in charge of the rear guard. The enemy having crossed, all his cavalry made a most determined effort to rout the rear guard, composed of Pettus's and Cummings's Brigades of Stephenson's Division, beginning about four miles north of Spring Hill. Here Chalmers's Cavalry was driven off from the two small infantry brigades, and they alone had to resist the terrible onslaught of Wilson's entire force. The rear guard, under Gen. Stephenson, formed three sides of a square, and slowly cut its way to the rear, being attacked in the front, flank, and rear, and keeping this up to within a short distance of Spring Hill. Here Clayton sent a brigade (Holtzclaw's) back to help, and formed his other two brigades across the pike to resist the cavalry, for Wilson had gotten between the two commands. There could not have been a more gallant effort to crush a rear guard of any retreating army than Wilson made, and certainly never did a rear guard perform its critical duty better. The two brigades numbered about 700 men. This was the afternoon after the great [Yankee] victory, and 12,000 [Union] cavalry were trying to ride over the devoted [Confederate] rear guard. This day's effort really saved Hood's army and gave an effectual check in pursuit, the effort extending into the night of December 17. Wilson did not again show such dash and boldness in pursuit. Gen. Lee relinquished his command during the night of the 17th, putting Gen. Stephenson in command of his corps.

On December 18 the cavalry of the enemy pursued continually to near Rutherford Creek, and on the 19th to Rutherford Creek, which was up and could not be crossed by the enemy, because their pontoon train was not up. Wilson's entire cavalry corps ceased pursuit on the evening of December 19, and went into camp, drawing supplies; nor did the enemy's cavalry renew pursuit till the morning of December 22, thus allowing Hood's army December 17, 18, 19, 20, and 21 to move steadily toward the Tennessee River. Hood's army crossed Duck River by the morning of December 20 at Columbia, and resumed retreat December 21. After Gen. Hood was safely over Duck River with his army, and the enemy's cavalry had ceased pursuit during December 19, 20, and 21, owing to high water in Rutherford Creek and the Union pontoon trains not being up, it gave him (Gen. Hood) a breathing spell, and the army had pretty well recovered from its rout

Stephen D. Lee, C.S.A.

and panic. Organizations had been perfected, and everything was ready to move slowly over the bad roads toward the Tennessee River December 21. Gen. Forrest, near Murfreesboro, heard of Gen. Hood's disaster before Nashville during the night of December 16, and under orders retreated in the direction of Columbia, on Duck River, to join Gen. Hood. He reached

Columbia with his command on the evening of December 18, and went into camp at Columbia on December 19. Some of the enemy's cavalry appeared before Columbia on the evening of December 20 in observation.

On December 20 Gen. Hood, before resuming his retreat, organized a strong rear guard composed of Gen. Forrest's Cavalry and five brigades of infantry under Gen. Walthall, the two commands being under command of Gen. Forrest. The enemy's cavalry crossed Duck River on December 22 and resumed pursuit. His infantry never pursued after December 17, and never came in contact with the rear of Hood's army. This rear guard was ably handled by Gen. Forrest, and presented such a bold front that Gen. Wilson showed but little disposition to press it, except at two points. On December 24 the whole cavalry corps of the enemy resumed pursuit, and attacked the rear guard under Forrest at Lynnville and was checked, and again below Pulaski, when Walthall, with his infantry, gave a decided check and captured a gun and prisoners. Wilson followed to Sugar Creek, and on December 27 saw the last of Hood's army across the Tennessee River.[24] — CONFEDERATE GENERAL STEPHEN DILL LEE

DEBUNKING ANOTHER YANKEE MYTH
☛ [In discussions of the Battle of Nashville] there is one expression sometimes used to which I wish to enter protest. It has been frequently said that when the [Confederate] line gave way at Shy's Hill a "panic" ensued and the entire army fled in disorderly rout, etc. There was no panic.

For two days the soldiers in Stewart's Corps had faced an enemy overwhelming in numbers, and with indomitable pluck had met and repelled every assault, all the time being conscious of the fact that their position was being turned and would finally become untenable. The lines were extended to the

Wilbur F. Foster, C.S.A.

left from time to time to meet this flanking movement of the enemy, always in the best of order and with unbroken front. On the second day, Cheatham's Corps, transferred to Stewart's left, confronted the same enveloping movement so well described [above] by Gen. [S. D.] Lee.

At last the crisis came, anticipated by everybody, when at about 4 P.M. on the 16th the Brentwood hills, in the rear of Cheatham's and Stewart's Corps, were being occupied by the enemy in strong force. Nobody knew better than the Confederate soldiers in the rifle pits that their line could be no longer maintained, and that only one outlet was open by which to escape inevitable capture. At that moment the line gave way at Shy's Hill, and

served as a signal for a stampede to the Franklin Turnpike. This was done, of course, in great disorder; but if "panic" was there, I failed to see it.

This writer was in the rush along the foot of the Brentwood hills, and well remembers certain jibes and sarcastic remarks of the men, but no cries of terror. The men simply knew, without being told, that there was but one thing to do, and that was to get to the Franklin Pike; and they did it, not because they were panic-stricken, but because it was the proper thing to do.[25] — CONFEDERATE MAJOR WILBUR F. FOSTER (engineer officer under Gen. Alexander P. Stewart)

A SOUTHERN HEROINE AT NASHVILLE
☞ The battle of Nashville gave us a heroine whose name General Hood placed on the roll of honor, "Miss Mary Bradford," now Mrs. John Johns. When Thomas' Army was pouring the musketry into us and Hood's Army was in full retreat, she rushed out in the thickest of the storm cloud and begged the soldiers to stop and fight.[26] — B. L. RIDLEY (Murfreesboro, Tenn.)

GENERAL SEARS & BILLY
☞ While there have been recorded in public print countless deeds of heroism and fortitude of the Confederate soldier, in my humble opinion none has surpassed that of Gen. Claudius W. Sears at the battle of Nashville, during Gen. Hood's Tennessee campaign. As I have never seen any reference to it in print, it gives me pleasure to save it from oblivion, and hence I write . . . of that gallant old Confederate soldier and his faithful horse Billy. I was present when it occurred.

The Federal forces had succeeded in turning the right and left wings of the Confederate army. Sears's Brigade occupied a central position, and when his command yielded to the inevitable it passed under fire from front, right, and left. After extricating his command from this position, Gen. Sears rode to a small eminence, in order to get a better view of the enemy. He removed his field glass from its case, and began his inspection. While seated upon his horse and with the glass to his eyes, the enemy fired a shell at him. It carried away one of his legs below the knee, and it also killed his horse.

The General was a man about sixty years of age, the ground was frozen hard and was covered with deep snow, and it seemed the coldest as well as the saddest day I had ever experienced. No surgeon was near to administer to his pressing need; everything was in confusion, and in the midst of all the sad surroundings and heartrending scenes of a fierce battle the grand old hero stood upon one foot, and, with tears running down his cheeks, like a child, exclaimed: "Poor Billy! Poor Billy!" He did not seem to notice his own sad condition, but his whole attention and sympathy were directed toward the faithful steed which he had ridden during the entire war.

An ambulance was secured to carry him off the field, and, after making him as comfortable as possible, we bade him adieu, never expecting to see him again. Many of us never did.

They say "fortune favors the brave." In this case it certainly did, for he recovered and was for many years professor of mathematics at the University of Mississippi. His son has presented his portrait to the Historical Committee of Mississippi, to be placed in the Hall of Fame at Jackson. There are few who are more worthy of this distinguished honor, and Mississippi in honoring him honors herself.[27] — CONFEDERATE SOLDIER R. N. REA (Brunette, La.)

LAST SHOTS AT THE BATTLE OF NASHVILLE

☛ When the Confederate lines gave way all was confusion and disorder. The boys up and down the line stood up in the ditches, adjusted their accouterments, and prepared for the race before them. The officers urged the men to remain in the ditches and wait for orders to leave. If the orders were given, I never heard them. I could see our lines giving way on our left, and all at once the entire line jumped out of the ditches and started on a disorderly though rapid run for the Franklin Pike, a mile away. I could see the Yankee columns flanking us on our left, and we all realized that we should soon be captured unless we saved ourselves by flight.

The ground was very muddy, and not a good race track, though we made very good time. The fall of Minie balls, accompanied by shell and grapeshot caused us to increase our speed. I passed our major general, Edward Johnston, who was on foot. He had left his horse for safety, and had gone in the line. Being very corpulent and unaccustomed to running, he was soon far behind. I overtook the orderly with the general's horse, but he refused to take the horse back. One daring fellow offered to do so, but the orderly would not release the animal, and the General was captured.

"All at once the entire line jumped out of the ditches and started on a disorderly though rapid run."

Just as I reached the Franklin Pike, at the foot of the mountain, some one with a [Confederate] battle flag waved it, crying: "Halt and rally round the flag, boys!" Soon there were several hundred of us formed in line across the pike, and we began firing at the bluecoats in the valley below. I don't think there were any officers present. It seemed to be a "private" affair, though "free for all."

This voluntary attempt to rally did but little good, but it checked the rapidly advancing column for a few moments, and enabled many exhausted Confederates to escape. We fired a few rounds—the last shots fired at the battle of Nashville—and when the enemy were getting uncomfortably close some one cried out: "It's no use, boys; let's give it up, or we will be captured," and all fell back in wild confusion.

Night was soon on us, and the road was fearfully muddy. We had no rations, and had gotten but little sleep for several nights. Tennesseans never had a more disagreeable night march. Thus in the midst of winter and but poorly clad we started into Hood's memorable retreat from Nashville, which lasted nearly a week, while the ever-vigilant Yanks were thundering in our rear day and night.[28] — AN UNNAMED CONFEDERATE SOLDIER

THE RETREAT FROM NASHVILLE

☛ About 11 a.m. [on December 16, 1864] the Louisiana Brigade was in position, our right resting on the Franklin pike. A brigade of negro troops [U.S.] made an assault on our line, but were soon badly demoralized by our fire. I sent out a detail of three men to capture the colors (we had no use for prisoners), and they returned with a handsome flag, on which was inscribed: "Presented by the Colored Ladies of Murfreesboro, Tenn." I gave it to the color bearer, and when Lieut. Gen. S. D. Lee came along he remarked on the handsome flag. He asked me to give three cheers, so it would go down the line and encourage the troops on our left wing.

While standing with Gen. Lee a ball went through the rim of my hat. Again while looking for sharpshooters a ball passed through my hat, coming out at the crown, and the third shot tore a V-shaped hole in the shoulder of my overcoat.

About three in the afternoon of that day I saw our men on the left giving way and the enemy sweeping up our line. Gen. Gibson ordered me to keep the trenches until we had orders to retreat. As I left the trench I met Gen. Edward Johnson running rapidly. He told me he was just from prison, and was too tired to go farther. Soon afterwards he was again a prisoner.

With my color bearer I made for the pike, where our horses were. The enemy had some guns, and swept lanes in which were the retreating Confederates. About dark Gibson's Louisiana Brigade formed the rear guard to protect our badly demoralized army. I quote from Gen. Lee's report of that evening: "At Nashville when Hood was defeated, Gibson's Brigade was conspicuously posted on the left of the pike near Overton Hill, and I witnessed their driving back with the rest of Clayton's Division two formidable assaults of the enemy. I recollect near dark riding up to a brigade near a battery and trying to seize a stand of colors and lead the brigade against the enemy. The color bearer refused, and was sustained by his regiment. I found it was the color bearer of the Thirteenth Louisiana

Volunteers and Gibson's Louisiana Brigade. Gibson soon appeared at my side, and in admiration of such conduct I exclaimed: "Gibson, these are the best men I ever saw. You take them and check the enemy." Gibson did take them, and did check the enemy.

The Harpeth River, Franklin, Tenn., key crossing point during Hood's Tennessee Campaign. (Photo Lochlainn Seabrook)

Hood, in his [book] *Advance and Retreat* gives to Gen. Gibson and his command the credit of staying the disorder in the army and stopping the panic. He says: "Gen. Gibson with the Louisiana troops succeeded in checking and staying the first and most dangerous shock which always follows immediately after a rout."

Gibson's Brigade and Fenner's Battery acted as rear guard to the rear guard (old soldiers will appreciate the meaning of those words), and continued as rear guard until relieved by Gen. [Lawrence S.] Ross and his cavalry.

When we reached Franklin the Louisiana Brigade formed line from pike to railroad and kept the enemy in check until all of our wounded and ammunition train safely crossed the Harpeth River, then the brigade turned in good order and formed line on the outskirts of Franklin, our right resting on the pike. Here it was Gen. Lee was wounded in the foot. After this the enemy became more cautious, and our army crossed the Tennessee River and went to Tupelo, Miss.[29] — COLONEL R. H. LINDSAY (16th Louisiana Regiment, Gibson's Brigade)

BEFORE & AFTER THE BATTLE OF NASHVILLE

☛ In retrospecting the past, the arduous duty of covering Hood's retreat from Tennessee looms up with vivid recollections of the hardships and dangers experienced by true men having it in charge.

The horrors of war had been focalized into one dense dark cloud over our heads for several days and nights, when ruin and annihilation seemed inevitable. We had hardly recuperated from the hundred days fighting between Dalton and Atlanta, which began May 7, 1864, at Ringgold, Ga., and ended at Lovejoy, Ga., below Atlanta, about the first of September. It was a harder campaign than the one under Gen. [Braxton] Bragg in the fall of 1862, beginning at Cumberland Gap, Tenn., and extending to Frankfort and Harrisburg, Ky., two hundred miles distance. Returning from that campaign, we arrived at Tazewell, Tenn., December 24, 1862, on Saturday night, when snow fell upon us to the depth of about eight inches. On the next Sunday, about eleven o'clock, we started for Vicksburg, Miss., getting there about noon on the 28th. We immediately got off the cars and double-quicked to the battle-field, Chickasaw Bayou, where a battle was already raging.

But I am rambling from the main thought. After the fight at Jonesboro we had a ten days' armistice, and then we started on the famous march under Gen. J. B. Hood [north] to Nashville. We went through part of Alabama, over Sand Mountain, then to Columbia, Tenn., at which place we encountered some Yankees, but they soon fell back to Franklin [a Confederate win]. As our command brought up the rear from Columbia, we did not get into the hardest fighting. About twelve o'clock that night we were put in the second line of the Yankee works, near the turnpike, to support our front line. Our men were on one side of the breastworks and the enemy on the other, from which position they retreated to within a few miles of Nashville. We pursued them, and established our line so close that we could not put out pickets in the daytime. There we remained some time, doing picket duty.

Forrest, with sword drawn, leading one of his many successful cavalry charges against the Yanks.

About the 5th of December it snowed, and when not on picket duty many of our boys had a big time catching rabbits. We were so close to the enemy that we had to move our line back so we could have fires, as it was very cold. One night while on vidette, with the snow and sleet about eight inches deep, I felt sure, from the noise in front, that a Yank was coming. I stood with my gun cocked, ready to shout at sight. Imagine my relief when I found it was no greater foe than Mr. Rabbit.

Soon thereafter the severe battle of Nashville was fought. Its results are ever vivid to participants.

When on retreat Gen. Hood told Gen. E. C. Walthall that Forrest said he could not keep the enemy without a strong infantry support, and he asked for three thousand infantry, with Gen. Walthall to command them. Gen. Walthall said he had never sought a hard place for glory nor a soft one for comfort, but took his chances as they came. When the order was given we saw the maneuvering of our troops, wondering what was up. Joe Parr, my messmate, said to me: "We are going to catch it." The rear-guard was composed of D. H. Reynolds', Featherston's, Smith's, Maney's, and Palmer's Brigades, numbering in all one thousand six hundred and one men. Imagine the privations we had on that retreat to the Tennessee River!

Gen. Thomas, the Federal commander, in his official report, said that Hood had formed a powerful rear-guard, made up of all organized forces, numbering four thousand infantry, with all the available cavalry under Forrest; that had it not been for this rear-guard Hood's army would have become a disorganized rabble; and that the rear-guard was undaunted and firm, and did its work bravely to the last.

A grand commander was Nathan Bedford Forrest, and this rear-guard to Hood's army on that retreat was worthy to be commanded by him.[30] — CONFEDERATE SOLDIER GEORGE I. C. MCWHIRTER (52nd Georgia Regiment)

AN ATTEMPT TO SAVE THE FEET OF HOOD'S SOLDIERS
☛ When Hood's army arrived before Franklin in November, 1864, it was by reason of its long, hurried march from Atlanta poorly equipped, especially as to clothing and shoes. Those who went through and survived the terrific battle of Franklin were indeed ragged, worn out, and suffering in body and mind, but still had the spirit of fight in them.

When the army arrived before Nashville, General Hood learned that down near the mouth of Duck River on the opposite side from his army there was located a large tannery and shoe manufacturing establishment operated by the United States government. As his army was suffering terribly for the want of shoes, it was very desirable to get hold of this factory and any leather and shoes that might be there before the Union forces abandoned and destroyed it. At that time it was expected that the Confederate army would capture and occupy Nashville.

Immediately on learning of the existence of this big tannery a young staff officer was detailed to go down and try to secure the tannery and leather that might be there and, if possible, start to making shoes. A company of cavalry was selected to go on this expedition, and splendid fellows they proved to be—young, but veterans in service, well mounted, and used to hardships.

A guide was procured and the company started at once; no wagons, no artillery, simply what they could carry on their horses in the way of rations, arms, and ammunition.

Arriving at Duck River somewhere near its mouth, the river was found to be greatly swollen by reason of heavy rains. No ferryboats or means of crossing could be found. The people living in the neighborhood welcomed the Confederates and did what they could for them. They told the young men that it was absolutely impossible to cross the stream in its present condition, it being so high and the current so strong and swift. Their advice was to go back; but the Confederates were not going to do that. They could give up their lives in doing their duty, and the young staff officer in charge of the expedition proposed that they swim the river on their horses. The natives said that it was impossible, that they would be swept out through the mouth of the river and drowned. Nevertheless, volunteers were called for to go into the river, and every fellow went. It was a perilous undertaking; but the horses as well as the men were used to dangers and difficulties.

Success crowned the efforts of the little company. They landed, but were scattered about along the bank of the river from a quarter to a half mile below where they went in, the swift current having swept every horse down the stream; but at last all landed safe, with guns and cartridges dry.

The tannery was soon located. Many rumors were heard about it, such as it being strongly guarded with a large force of Union troops, while other reports were to the effect that it had been abandoned. The little command of Confederates, however, rushed on, really hoping to find

The Duck River, Columbia, Tenn., another crucial transit location that greatly influenced both armies during the fighting in Middle Tennessee. (Photo Lochlainn Seabrook)

some troops still there on guard. It was believed that if the tannery had been abandoned it would also be destroyed. They preferred to fight and capture it rather than get there too late. It was but a few miles to the tannery, and it was found to be all complete, having just been abandoned. No shoes were there, but there were many pieces of leather, and steps were being taken to begin the manufacture of some kind of foot covering to answer as shoes for the barefooted boys in front of Nashville.

Before this was actually begun, however, orders were received to return immediately and join Hood's army as it fell back. The battle of Nashville had been fought and lost, and the army was in retreat. With grief and sorrow we prepared to go. A roll of leather was tied to each saddle, knowing that even this would be of immense value to the men if time could be found to turn it into shoes of some kind.

The company went back and joined the army on its retreat; and as the men marched down the pike, many of them barefooted, with feet bleeding, a part of the way over snow, the regret as to not having had the time to use the splendid tannery grew more bitter. But those were days when Confederates had to meet with many disappointments.

This episode is given as I remember it after these many years. I have not met since then any one who was on that raid, and I have sometimes wondered as my mind has often dwelt upon it if I were not dreaming. I do not know what company of cavalry it was, but the officer in command of it told me that it was a Tennessee company, recruited from around Memphis, and I think he stated that it was Forrest's original company.

. . . The retreat from Nashville was one of the most heroic and orderly of which history gives any account. The advance of the Union army frequently found when they came to our rear guard that there was plenty of fight left in us.[31] — CONFEDERATE CAPTAIN A. C. DANNER (Mobile, Ala.)

THE CONFEDERATE RETREAT FROM NASHVILLE

☞ When the [final Confederate] line gave way, Cheatham dispatched a staff officer to the commanding general, to report the condition of the left and to ask that some body of troops should be halted east of the Granny White pike to cover the withdrawal of his left. There was no panic there, but he decided not to attempt to bring out the organizations, and directed the men to retire without order and cross the hills to the Franklin road. [Mark P.] Lowrey's and [Hiram B.] Granbury's brigades of Cheatham's division, under Brig.-Gen. A. J. Smith, who had been sent in the forenoon to support the center, were ordered back to the left just as the disaster occurred, halted and put into position, and they checked the advance of the enemy long enough to enable the troops on the extreme left to retire in safety. Brig.-Gens. Henry R. Jackson and Thomas B. Smith, Bate's division, were not affected by the panic and were captured. Col. M. Mageveny, Jr., One Hundred and Fifty-fourth Tennessee, unable to climb the hills when his regiment was ordered to retire, was captured, and the gallant Col. William W. Shy, Twentieth Tennessee, was killed.

The casualties were inconsiderable in numbers. *There was no serious resistance to the Federal advance; it was a battle without an engagement or a contest; and the wonder is that Thomas, with a large and well-appointed army, more than treble the strength of Hood, did not press his right, seize the Franklin turnpike and capture the entire army.* Hood's army was in a wretched state, the clothing of the men was scant, and the percent of the barefooted was distressing. On the retreat out of Tennessee the weather was very severe, rain, sleet and snow falling upon the army after the second day's march; but the spirit of endurance seemed to rise as difficulties multiplied.

Maj.-Gen. George H. Thomas in his official report says of Hood's army: "With the exception of his rear guard, his army had become a disheartened and disorganized rabble of half-armed and barefooted men, who sought every opportunity to fall out by the wayside and desert their cause to put an end to their suffering. The rear guard, however, was undaunted and firm, and did its work bravely to the last." This report was prepared more than a month after the battle, and assumed to be historically correct.

. . . It was evident that while we had large numbers of poorly-clad and barefooted men, the accusation that they "sought every opportunity to fall out by the wayside and desert their cause" was *without foundation.*

Immediately after the break in our line the troops sought their own organizations, reformed under their officers, and marched out of the State in perfect order. The formation was made just south of the hills in the rear of our left, a few hundred yards from the abandoned line of battle, where, *on account of the timid policy of the Federal commander, and his proverbial want of enterprise, our army was not molested.* The men, with an occasional exception, had arms in their hands. At Franklin there were several thousand stand of arms, a very large proportion captured from the enemy; and after the loss of fifty pieces of artillery, the [Confederate] army retired with fifty-nine field pieces and an ample supply of ammunition. The successful resistance to the assault of the Federal cavalry near Franklin by the rear guard of Lee's corps [the Battle of Franklin III], repeated at Spring Hill the next day by the rearguard of Cheatham's corps, does not sustain the Federal general's report that our army was a "disorganized rabble."

While disasters had multiplied and the suffering was great, the spirit of the men was unbroken. It was well illustrated by Colonel Kellar, Fourth Tennessee, who in his report to Hood said: "For the first time in this war we lost our cannon. Give us the first chance and we will retake them." In the loss of artillery at Nashville, that of three 12-pounder Napoleon guns by Turner's Mississippi battery caused infinite regret in Cheatham's division. With other pieces they had been captured at Perryville, and had been served in all the subsequent battles of the Southwest with the greatest distinction by the company of noble Mississippians who manned them.

William W. Loring, C.S.A.

General Hood had been over-confident and too enthusiastic. When he retreated from Nashville his only hope was to save the remnant of his army, and he looked to the indomitable Forrest to accomplish this result. The cavalry had suffered from constant exposure to the trying winter weather and was not in condition unaided to check the advance of the enemy long enough to secure Hood's retreat, therefore it was decided to detach Major-General Walthall with instructions to organize a rear guard 3,000 strong, and report to Major General Forrest. Walthall selected the brigades of Reynolds, Ector and Quarles, of his own division; Featherston's, of Loring's division; Carter's (formerly Maney's), of Cheatham's division,

Among other damage, Forrest destroyed 36 railroad bridges, 200 miles of railroad, 6 engines, 100 cars, and $15,000,000 worth of Yankee property—in less than a year.

commanded by Col. H. R. Feild; Strahl's, of Cheatham's division, commanded by Col. C. H. Heiskell, and Smith's, of Cleburne's division. Instead of 3,000 men, the effective total was 1,601, but it was a splendid command, led with consummate skill and courage. "Walthall was the youngest division general in the army of Tennessee, and when he drew his sword in command over the rear guard to cover its retreat, there was not a soldier in it, from the commanding general down, who did not believe he would do it or perish in the effort." General Forrest said of him: "He exhibited the highest soldierly qualities; many of his men were without shoes, but they bore their sufferings without murmur, and were ever ready to meet the enemy."

General Walthall said of his command, "For several days the ground was covered with snow, and numbers of the men made the march without shoes, some had no blankets, and all were poorly clad for the season"; but despite these difficulties and privations there was no complaint. Every day there was a skirmish or a combat, in which the cavalry and artillery of Forrest participated with the infantry of Walthall. The danger was a common one, and the two arms of the service were alike conspicuous for courage and endurance. The Federal advance was beaten and punished day by day so thoroughly that General Thomas was forced to admit that "the rear guard was undaunted and firm, and did its work bravely to the last." The rear guard recrossed the Tennessee [River] on the 27th of December, Ector's brigade under Col. D. Coleman, Thirty-ninth North Carolina, in the rear.

General Forrest, in his report of the campaign, said that from the 21st of November to the 27th of December his command was engaged every day with the enemy. "I brought out three pieces of artillery (taken from the enemy), more than I started with. My command captured and destroyed 16 blockhouses and stockades, 20 bridges, 4 locomotives, 100 cars, 10 miles of railroad, and have turned over to the provost-marshal 1,600 prisoners, besides the capture of several hundred horses, mules and cattle." In an address to his troops issued by Forrest on his return to Corinth, Miss., he said: "During the past year (1864) you have fought 50 battles, killed and captured 16,000 of the enemy, captured 2,000 mules and horses, 67 pieces of artillery, 4 gunboats, 14 transports, 20 barges, 300 wagons, 50 ambulances, 10,000 stand of small-arms, 40 blockhouses, destroyed 36 railroad bridges, 200 miles of railroad, 6 engines, 100 cars, and $15,000,000 worth of (Federal) property [the equivalent of $302 million in today's currency]. Your strength never exceeded 5,000, 2,000 of whom have been killed or wounded; in prisoners you have lost about 200."

This summary of his operations doubtless stimulated General Sherman to advise the assassination of Forrest and to commit other atrocities. An order, or letter of instructions, dated Savannah, Ga., January 21, 1865, addressed to Gen. George H. Thomas, giving "such instructions as fall within my province as commander of the division," General Sherman advised him to march on Columbus, Miss., Tuscaloosa and Selma, "destroying farms, gathering horses, mules (wagons to be burned), and doing all possible damage, burning Selma and Montgomery, Ala., and all iron foundries, mills and factories," and adds: "I would like to have Forrest hunted down and killed, but doubt if we can do that yet." *If the Spanish Captain-General [Valeriano] Weyler, of Cuba, had issued and published this letter of instructions to a subordinate officer, the press, the pulpit, the halls of Congress of the United States would have rung with fierce denunciation of the savage spirit of its author, and public opinion would outlaw his memory.*

The remnant of the army of Tennessee retired from Corinth to Tupelo, Miss., on the 23rd of January, 1865. General Hood was relieved and Lieut.-Gen. Richard Taylor assigned to command.[32] — CONFEDERATE OFFICER JAMES DAVIS PORTER (Chief of Staff under Gen. Cheatham)

ECTOR'S BRIGADE IN THE BATTLE OF NASHVILLE

☛ Ector's Brigade was composed of the Tenth, Fourteenth, and Thirty-Second Texas and the Twenty-Ninth and Thirty-Ninth North Carolina Regiments. Gen. Ector having lost a leg at Atlanta in July, the brigade was commanded by the senior colonel, Col. Coleman, Thirty-Ninth North Carolina.

"We gave the enemy a warm reception."

On the morning of December 15 the brigade was camped on Harding Pike, with a picket line in front, extending across the pike at the mouth of a lane, in charge of Capt. House, of the Tenth, on the right and the writer on the left. We soon discovered a vast body of [Union] cavalry maneuvering to our left front, and a little later we saw a large brigade of infantry advancing upon our left front in line of battle, followed by a battery of artillery. We reported to Col. Coleman, who came to our line and examined the situation. He instructed us to hold the line until forced to retire, then to fall back over the ridge in order, and make a run of about two miles to the Hillsboro Pike, where we would find him with the brigade.

The enemy threw forward a skirmish line and moved slowly but steadily forward. Our thin line in rifle pits gave them a warm reception. When they got uncomfortably near, we hastily fell back, but in order, over the ridge. We then made a run for the brigade, fearful of being cut off by cavalry.

We found the brigade near the Hillsboro Pike in line of battle fronting west. Very soon a large regiment of cavalry galloped up in our front to the foot of the hill, probably a hundred yards distant, and halted Col. Coleman, called to them to show their colors, for as the morning was gloomy he could not determine whether they were Federals or Confederates, but they made no response. Then Col. Coleman gave the command to fire. They returned the fire, but soon retreated at full speed. Their loss was pretty heavy, especially in horses killed. If we had any loss, I did not hear of it.

In another minute or two our brigade was ordered into a redoubt near the pike. About this time we heard a heavy battle in front and to our right. Very soon we could see the Confederate lines moving to the rear and to our right, but fighting desperately as they retreated. They and the Federals, that were pressing them, passed our fort and left us in the rear. A prompt retreat was ordered, and we moved at a double quick on a line parallel with the movement of the troops in the battle.

When we got to the Brentwood range of hills, Gen. Hood and his staff were on the hill. Gen. Hood rode down the line saying to all the soldiers as he passed, "Texans, I want you to hold this hill regardless of what transpires around you," and the spontaneous answer was: "We will do it, General."

Our line was formed on the brow of the hill fronting west. In the meantime the battle reported above had ceased and Gen. Bate was re-forming his lines to our right and in plain view of our line. Soon they attacked him again, and for a time we stood watching a terrific battle. A battery of artillery close in the rear of Bate's Infantry on a little eminence did splendid work. The lines of infantry wavered back and forth as long as we saw the fight. Before very long, however, a strong force of infantry attacked our line and made a desperate, but unsuccessful, effort to drive us from the hill. Night closed the conflict with our line unmoved. Our losses were pretty heavy. During the night our brigade was relieved by other troops and placed on the east side of the hill in reserve. By morning the troops that took our place had very good fortifications.

On the 16th, from our position on the side of the hill overlooking the

Granny White Pike at a point where the road makes a right-angle turn to the east, we could plainly see the assaults made upon Lee's line. About noon one (Ector's) brigade was ordered to the left, nearly due south, at a double-quick, to head off a flank movement of the enemy over the range of hills. When we arrived at the place, their skirmish line was in possession of the hill, but we climbed the hill, which was very steep, and drove them off. We held this hill till late in the evening, when we were ordered down to an old country road running down the narrow valley. When we got to this road we found a column of troops marching in quick step down the valley, when we learned that Hood's entire army was in full retreat, and we were ordered to follow.

A pontoon bridge, this one spanning the Tennessee River at Decatur, Ala., 1864.

Soon a brigade of Federals attacked our retreating column from the west, and Ector's Brigade was called on to drive them back, which was done by a vigorous charge just at twilight. We hastily gathered up our wounded and carried them to some farmhouses near by and continued our march, intersecting the Franklin Pike, which we found full of retreating troops.

We had no more fighting till we got to Columbia [46 miles South of Nashville]. At this point Ector's Brigade and four other little decimated brigades under Gen. Walthall were attached to Forrest's Cavalry, constituting the rear guard of the army to the Tennessee River. Of all the hard service poor soldiers ever endured, this is among the worst.

On Christmas day we left Pulaski, setting fire to the bridge there when we left. The rascals [Yankees] came up, put the fire out, and crossed over and attacked us on the first hill. We gave them a good drubbing, however, capturing some of their artillery. We made a forced march then to Sugar Creek, only a few miles from the Tennessee River, wading the creek in a late hour of the night and bivouacked at the edge of the valley, half a mile or more from the creek.

At daylight we were aroused and informed that the Yankees were on our side of the creek. A dense fog rested upon the valley. After waiting some time for them to make an attack, which they failed to do, we were ordered to charge them, and did it very successfully. In trying to cross the creek on their big cavalry horses, the banks on our side were so high they could not ascend them, and our boys captured many large, fine horses. When they were driven across the creek, Gen. Ross's Cavalry Brigade charged and drove them for miles. Our brigade got a good Yankee breakfast from the saddle pockets on horses killed and captured. From there to the pontoon bridge on the Tennessee River our brigade was largely mounted.[33]
—CONFEDERATE LIEUTENANT J. T. TUNNELL (14th Texas Infantry)

GEN. LEE'S PART IN CHECKING THE CONFEDERATE RETREAT

☛ As far as I have been able to read, the time which elapsed between the rout of Hood's army, on the afternoon of the 16th of December, 1864, and that when said army reached Brentwood, a station four miles to the rear of the battlefield, has been left a comparative blank, and what occurred during that short period has been entirely overlooked, to the detriment of a man who was and is every inch a soldier, a perfect type of the American Anglo-Saxon, beloved of his men, and freely spoken of by them in time of war as one of the bravest men in the army, a general among generals.

. . . I refer as a personal witness, even though a humble Confederate private, to the time when, about four o'clock in the afternoon of December 16, Gen. Stephen D. Lee formed a rear guard for Hood's defeated army by his own heroic efforts, and continued in command of that rear guard all of the night of the 16th and all of the day of the 17th. After being wounded on the 17th, he continued in command of the rear guard until nightfall. When he was physically unable to further remain in command, he turned over a well-organized rear guard to Maj. Gen. Stevenson.

I remember as if it were only yesterday the morning of the 16th of December, 1864. The morning opened silent and murky. Not a gun was heard, although everybody expected that the battle would begin quickly, for the Federal lines were drawn up and almost in front of the thin Confederate line, which had sustained defeat on the day before in front of Nashville and had fallen back to a new line, with Lee's Corps to the right and on or near Overton's Hill.

The Confederate army was stretched in a single line of battle. In some places the men were fully five feet apart, while here and there a single company of infantry was placed in the rear to support and reenforce such parts of it as might need their services. It was, in fact, only a good skirmish line, although the remnant of Hood's army—after the disastrous battle of Franklin and the engagement of the day before (December15). Gen. Lee literally opened the fight by exposing himself. He rode to the left of his corps, and then rode down the line of battle, followed by his staff and couriers. As he passed each Federal battery he was given a full discharge of the battery. By the time he had ridden down his line, the battle was in full progress, and very soon the charging began, and it continued all day at intervals until about four o'clock in the afternoon. Every charge made by the Federals in front of Lee was repulsed, and in some instances the Confederates sprang over their temporary breastworks and met the enemy, who were charging, capturing numbers of stands of colors.

Stephen D. Lee, C.S.A.

I was with Gen. Lee at the time the line broke. We were mounted sitting just in the rear of a Confederate battery and of Clayton's Division. Over on the left we could see confusion, and we saw a Federal line advancing from the rear and attacking the left wing of Lee's Corps. Everything else had apparently been swept before it. Clayton's Division was divided by the Franklin pike. Gen. Lee rode across the pike, taking both stone fences, followed by Maj. Ratchford, of his staff, and by Robert Howard and myself, of his escort. He rode until he reached the rear of Stevenson's Division of his corps, rode right into the midst of fugitives and in the face of the enemy, who by this time had reached the rear of Pettus's Brigade. Gen. Lee seized a stand of colors from a color bearer and carried it on horseback, making himself a conspicuous object for the Federal infantry. His example was inspiring. He looked like a very god of war. I recall his words as if only yesterday. They seemed to come from his very soul, as if his heart were breaking. One appeal was: "Rally, men, rally for God's sake, rally! This is the place for brave men to die!"

To those who came in contact with him and under the spell of his presence and personal magnetism the effect was electrical. Men gathered in little knots of four and five, prompted by individual gallantry. He soon had around him other stands of colors, three besides himself carried on horseback—one by his adjutant general, Maj. Ratchford, one by Robert Howard, and another by one of his couriers.

The Federals, meeting with this resistance, hesitated, halted. They were led by an officer on horseback, with a flag in his hand. I think he was wounded and fell to the ground. At any rate, if he was not killed it was not because he was not shot at often enough. I think his falling aided in checking the advance. This was late in the evening, and it was misty. The rally thus made enabled Clayton's Division to form a nucleus, and they, together with other Confederates, principally Lee's Corps, formed a line of battle. Gen. Lee came back from his advanced position to this line, which was formed on one of the Overton hills and crossing the Franklin pike. In order to reassure the men, Gen. Lee gave them the command to commence firing by file. I heard him afterwards say that he thought this would give them more confidence.

Of all our artillery, over one hundred pieces, only a few pieces joined this little band and commenced firing. Right at the wheel of one piece of artillery I recollect a [Confederate] drummer stood, a mere boy, and beat long roll in perfect time, without missing a note. The line of battle formed across the pike was a memorable one. It was certainly a brilliant array of colors, and struck me as a rally of color bearers. This line was in the woods, near Col. Overton's house, and was formed by Gen. R. L. Gibson, of Lee's Corps, under his direction. A little farther back, Maj. Gen. Clayton re-formed his division of Lee's Corps. This division and Gibson's Brigade and other troops continued to retreat until they reached Hollow Tree Gap, just north of Franklin, where they went into bivouac. This movement was all made under the direction of Gen. Lee.

Gen. Hood, in his official report of January 9, 1865, uses the following language: "At Brentwood, some four miles from our line of battle, the troops were somewhat collected, and Lieut. Gen. Lee took command of the rear guard, encamping for the night in that vicinity."

It is well known that Gen. Hood entertained the highest regard for Gen. Lee's ability. In his book, *Advance and Retreat*, he uses this language: "I might assert with equal assurance that, had Lieut. Gen. Lee been in advance at Spring Hill the previous afternoon, Schofield's army would never have passed that point." I merely mention this extract to show his exalted opinion of Gen. Lee.[34]

Gen. Hood fails to record the fact that Gen. Lee had checked the advance of the Federal army and had formed a rear guard before Brentwood was reached. It is this period of time, commencing between three and four o'clock in the afternoon, with the rout of Hood's army and its falling back to Brentwood, that history has been so silent in regard to Gen. Lee and his conspicuous gallantry in saving the remnant of Hood's army.

Gen. Hood, in *Advance and Retreat*, says: "Order among the troops was in a measure restored at Brentwood, a few miles in the rear of the scene of disaster, through the promptness and gallantry of Clayton's Division, which speedily formed and confronted the enemy, with Gibson's Brigade and McKenzie's Battery of Fenner's Battalion acting as rear guard of the rear guard. Gen Clayton displayed admirable coolness and courage that afternoon and next morning in the discharge of his duties. Gen. Gibson, who evinced conspicuous gallantry and ability in the handling of his troops, succeeded, in concert with Clayton, in checking and staying the first and most dangerous shock that always follows immediately after a rout. The result was that after the army passed the Big Harpeth [River] at Franklin the brigades and divisions were in marching order. Capt. Cooper, of my staff, had been sent to Murfreesboro to inform Gen. Forrest of our misfortune and to order him to make the necessary disposition of his cavalry to cover our retreat."

I was present and within pistol shot of Gen. Lee during the whole afternoon. I had been ordered by him to remain with him, having his field glasses in my possession, and I know of my own personal knowledge that no officer from Gen. Hood approached Gen. Lee with an order, nor was there any cavalry, of any command, on the battlefield within sight of Lee's Corps or of Gen. Lee. It was Gen. Lee's prompt action in rushing to the rear of Stevenson's Division and rallying the men in the face of the enemy that created the idea of organized resistance in the minds of the Federals and caused them to halt, thus giving Clayton's Division and some of the

Henry D. Clayton, C.S.A.

brigades of Stevenson's Division time to fall to the rear in comparatively good order and form, under the direction of Gen. Lee. But for this action on the part of Gen. Lee, the Federals, who were advancing on the left flank and rear of our army in a full run, would have been on all the troops of Clayton's Division in the rear before they would have had knowledge of their approach or time to get out in any order. The real rally took place on the left of the pike, in the rear of Stevenson's Division, and prior to the formation by Gen. Gibson of the troops above referred to on the right of the pike and in the rear of where Gen. Lee was checking the enemy. These facts doubtless were never brought to the attention of Gen. Hood. Gen. Lee, in his official report, fails signally to refer to them.

In Gen. Lee's official report of January 30, 1865, he refers to the rout in these words: "The troops along the entire line were in fine spirit and confident of success, so much so that the men could hardly be prevented from leaving their trenches to follow the enemy on and near the Franklin pike (he refers to the enemy who had charged his lines and been repulsed—CV editor); but suddenly all eyes were turned to the center of our line of battle, near the Granny White pike, where it was evident that the enemy had made an entrance, although but little firing had been heard in that direction. Our men were flying to the rear in the wildest confusion, and the enemy following with enthusiastic cheers. The enemy at once closed toward the gap in our line and commenced charging on the left division (Johnson's) of my corps, but were handsomely driven back. The enemy soon gained our rear and were moving on my left flank when our line gradually gave way. My troops left their lines in some disorder; but were soon rallied, and presented a good front to the enemy. It was a fortunate circumstance that the enemy were too much crippled to pursue us on the Franklin pike. The only pursuit at that time was by a small force coming from the Granny White pike."

Gen. Lee says his troops were soon rallied. Yes, indeed, they were. But who rallied them? On this point Gen. Lee is silent with his accustomed modesty. He caused them to present a good front to the enemy. Let justice be done even at this late day. There is not a living man who can deny that Gen. Stephen D. Lee rallied these troops, and to him belongs the credit of saving Hood's army.

Farther on in Gen. Lee's report, he says: "Being charged with covering the retreat of the army, I remained in the rear with Clayton's and a part of Stevenson's Division, and halted the rear guard about seven miles north of Franklin at about 10 P.M. on the 16th."

Gen. Forrest did not rejoin Hood's army until the evening of the 18th of December, near Columbia, about forty miles from Nashville, at which time he reported to Gen. Hood and was assigned to command the rear guard of the Army of Tennessee, Gen. Stephen D. Lee, who up to that time had commanded the rear guard, which he personally organized, having to retire from its command by reason of a serious wound. It was customary in the Army of Tennessee to alternate the different army corps in marching front, middle, and rear. Gen. Lee had been marching in the rear with his corps from the 16th of December up to and including the 18th of December. His corps then assumed the position as the center corps of the army, and Stewart's Corps, which by this time had been organized and was in good fighting shape, was placed in the rear.

This is the rear guard referred to by Gen. Thomas, of the Federal army, in his report: "Forrest and his cavalry and such other detachments as had been sent from Hood's main army joined Hood at Columbia. He formed a powerful rear guard, numbering about four thousand infantry and all his available cavalry. With the exception of this rearguard, his army had become a disheartened and disorganized rabble of half-armed and barefooted men. The rear guard, however, was undaunted and firm, and did its work bravely to the last."

That this rear guard, which took its place in the rear at Columbia, did its duty, no one will deny. It was commanded by Gen. Walthall, of

Stewart's Corps.

In *The Life of Gen. Forrest*, so beautifully written by John Allen Wyeth, it is stated that Gen. Forrest proposed to Gen. Hood to undertake the protection of his rear and requested that Maj. Gen. E. C. Walthall be placed at the head of the infantry, to act under his orders during the retreat, and he speaks of this rear guard as "the ever famous," and says that when the uncomplaining sacrifices which these heroic spirits made are fully known the historian and the poet will transmit to posterity in lasting form the thrilling story of the immortal rear guard of Hood's army under Forrest and Walthall."

Dr. Wyeth . . . [also] uses the following language: "Gen. Stephen D. Lee, who handled his corps with such marked ability and success in the two days battle in front of Nashville, still held his immediate command together in excellent fighting shape, and, selecting two brigades (Pettus's, of Alabama, and Stovall's, of Georgia) of troops, he, with the cavalry of Chalmers and Buford, organized these into a temporary rear guard and awaited the onslaught of the Union cavalry."

John A. Wyeth, C.S.A.

In a book recently published by Prof. John W. Burgess, of Columbia University, New York, I am sustained entirely in my position that it was the individual gallantry of Gen. Stephen D. Lee that saved the Army of Tennessee on the occasion referred to. In . . . describing the rout of Hood's army, he says: "The Confederates were now routed all along the line, and a scene of confusion and flight followed. Only the corps commander, Gen. Stephen D. Lee, stood and rallied around himself a handful of brave men and formed a rear guard to protect the retreat."

One of the participants in this engagement. Col. William Garrard, of Savannah, a lieutenant, and afterwards captain in Gen. Pettus's Brigade, and at that time serving on his staff, in a recent letter says: "We received the charge of the Federal cavalry with our two very small brigades, and repulsed them. We then began our retreat, throwing back the right regiment of our brigade and the left regiment of the Georgia Brigade, thus forming three sides of a square. We marched in this formation some time, facing outward when the Federal cavalry would charge us, which they did from time to time; and finally we threw a line across the rear of the square, reducing our frontage accordingly. This formed a hollow square, with our commanding officers, staffs, and couriers in the center. This formation was kept up during the day, the Federal cavalry attacking us repeatedly and always being repulsed. Our march during the day was across open fields covered with snow. In some places the men would sink up to their knees in mud and slush. There was nothing to do but fight, which was done most gallantly."

These are the troops that used this hollow square formation in battle, possibly the only time it has ever been used in America, that Gen. Thomas speaks of as "a disorganized rabble." This was Lee's rear guard, and it was in recognition of the gallant conduct of these troops that Gen. Lee, on December 18, while about to yield the command of his corps to Gen. Stevenson, on account of his severe wound received the day before, issued General Order No. 67: "Headquarters Lee's Corps, In the Field, Dec. 18, 1864. Before taking temporary leave of this corps, I desire

Carter L. Stevenson, C.S.A.

to express to the officers and men of my command my high appreciation of the good conduct and gallantry displayed by them at Nashville in the engagement of the 16th inst., and to assure them that they can be held in no manner responsible for the disaster of that day. I extend to them all my thanks for the manner in which they preserved their organization in the midst of temporary panic, rallying to their colors and presenting a determined front to the enemy, thus protecting the retreat of the army. I would also respectfully thank the officers and men of Holtzclaw's and Gibson's Brigades, of Clayton's Division, and of Pettus's Brigade, of Stevenson's Division, for the gallantry and courage with which they met and repulsed repeated charges of the enemy upon their line, killing and wounding large numbers of the assailants and causing them to retreat in confusion. I desire also to tender my heartfelt thanks to Maj. Gen. Stevenson and the officers and men of Pettus's and Cummings's Brigades, of his division, for their skillful, brave, and determined conduct while protecting the retreat of the army from Franklin yesterday. Constantly attacked in front and on either flank, these brave troops maintained an unshaken line, repulsed incessant attacks, and inflicted heavy loss. In conclusion, my brave comrades, I beg to assure you that I am not only satisfied with your conduct in the recent campaign, but that I shall repose unalterable confidence in you in the future—a future which, despite the clouds which seem to lower around us, will yet be rendered bright by the patriotic deeds of our gallant army, in which none will gain prouder laurels or do more gallant deeds than the veterans whom I have the honor to command. S. D. Lee. Lieutenant General."

I commenced this paper with a view to doing justice to Gen. Lee. I have long desired to see him given the credit for his glorious conduct, not only on the battlefield on the 16th of December, 1864, but during the time subsequent thereto, when Hood's army was in deadly peril, during which time he was in sole charge of the rear guard, of his own formation.[35] — CONFEDERATE PRIVATE LOUIS F. GARRARD (Columbia, Ga.)

LUMSDEN'S BATTERY AT THE BATTLE OF NASHVILLE

☛ Capt. Charles L. Lumsden was a graduate of the Virginia Military Institute, and at the outbreak of the war was military instructor of the corps of cadets at the University of Alabama. Under authority of the Confederate War Department he organized a battery of light artillery, all the officers and men volunteering from Tuscaloosa County, Ala., and served throughout the war. But it is only of the part this battery played at the battle of Nashville that I write; and be it understood that the writer was only a sergeant who, during most of the fight, was handling the trail of the fourth gun of the battery, aiming it at the enemy, while the cannoneers were doing their part loading and firing.

Drawing by artist Edwin Forbes of a 12 pound brass Napoleon gun, dated August 27, 1863.

Gen. Hood's line extended from about the Nashville and Chattanooga Railroad on the right to a little beyond the Hillsboro Pike on the left, about three and a half miles from Nashville. From the left of Hood's line to the Cumberland River, below Nashville, there were several miles of farming country crossed by the Harding and Charlotte Pikes, which were picketed by Gen. Chalmers's Cavalry, of about one thousand men, and Ector's Skeleton Brigade, seven or eight hundred strong. Gen. Hood had ordered five redoubts to be built to protect his left; three of them at the end just in rear of his intrenched line and the other two about a mile in rear of his extreme left, the troops occupying these latter two being ordered to "hold them at all hazards." These two redoubts were numbered four and five.

About December 9 Lumsden's Battery was ordered to occupy Redoubt No. 4. The battery consisted of four twelve pound smoothbore Napoleon guns that at six or eight hundred yards could be used with fair accuracy. Arriving at our position, we found that a slight trench, indicating the position of the guns and with a shallow ditch on either side for the infantry that were to support us, was all the fortifications that had been made. The weather was extremely cold from the 9th to the 14th: snow, sleet, and ice, with the ground frozen every morning. With a few old picks, shovels, and axes we succeeded in getting up breastworks in our immediate front, perhaps some seven feet high, with embrasures for the guns. All the horses, except one or two for courier work, were sent to the rear in charge of Lieut. Caldwell and the drivers, and we were then "ready for action."

There were present for duty Capt. Lumsden, Lieuts. E. H. Hargrove and A. C. Hargrove, Orderly Sergeant Mack Shivers, Sergeants James Jones, John Little, James Cardwell, and J. R. Maxwell [the writer of this article] in charge of the first, second, third, and fourth pieces, respectively, with a complement of one gunner and nine cannoneers to each piece, making a total of forty-eight men, rank and file. One hundred infantry, under Capt. John A. Foster, of the Twenty-Ninth Alabama, was our support, and were in the ditches on each side of the battery. These ditches were about two feet deep.

The sleet and snow had melted by the morning of the 15th and a heavy fog concealed everything. Scattering shots and an occasional wounded man coming from the front told us that the enemy was on the move around Hood's left flank. Gen. Thomas, in command of the Federal army, moved out from his right with the Fifth Division of his Cavalry Corps, Gen. Hatch commanding, with two brigades of four regiments each, supported by Knipe's Division of Cavalry in reserve, while A. J. Smith's Corps was the right wing of his infantry.

Gen. Chalmers's one thousand Confederate cavalry was first struck on Richland Creek by Hatch, who had dismounted six of his eight regiments, and driven back rapidly. Smith's Infantry Corps, pivoting opposite Hood's left, made a left wheel with a thick cloud of skirmishers in front, driving back Ector's Skeleton Brigade, which had been extended until they were nothing more than a thin skirmish line. It was about 11 a.m. when Ector's men passed us in retreat, going on both sides of our battery, leaving the bushy hollow in our front and to our right front full of Federal sharpshooters. Capt. Lumsden called to the officer to rally his men and help us hold our position, stating that we were ordered to hold it at all hazards. "It can't be done, sir; there is a whole army in your front," was the reply, and away they went.

About this time our part of the game opened. Three eight-gun batteries took position on a ridge about six hundred yards from us and opened fire on our battery. "Cannoneers, to your posts! Load shell six hundred yards!

Battery, ready! Fire!" were Capt. Lumsden's orders, and at it we went with four smooth bore guns behind the slight breastworks mentioned against twenty-four rifled pieces.

Corporal Ed King, of my gun, soon got the range, but was wounded by a splinter, and I was ordered to "take the trail." This suited me, for I had been gunner during the whole year's work, from Dalton to Atlanta, and was glad to get back in my old place again. The dirt, chunks, and stones were knocked in showers about us by the twenty-four guns of the enemy. For two hours we kept up the fight with that Yankee battery. Twice Capt. Lumsden had sent word back to Gen. Stewart telling him the situation: that a charge would sweep us off at any moment. The only reply was, "Hold them back as long as you can." It was about one o'clock when suddenly, and square off to our left about five hundred yards, another Federal four-gun battery opened on us, completely enfilading our position. My gun, being our left piece, was ordered to open on it, and the next gun to me was withdrawn sufficiently from the embrasure to give it range across the rear of my piece, and with solid shot we began to pound them. It was not long before we drove them off and again turned our attention to those in front. In whirling my gun back I broke off the rear pointing ring on the trail, but quickly looping it with a trace I soon had her "barking" again through the embrasure.

Just then Private Horton, No. 3 of my gun, went down, with a shot in his groin; he was carried to the rear, and that night we buried the poor fellow near the Franklin Pike. Helm Rosser, a lad of seventeen, the youngest of three brothers that belonged to the battery, had his head shot off by a shell, scattering his brains in the face of Capt. Lumsden. Shortly after this the captain shouted: "Look out, men! Give them canister!" They had, unobserved, worked around our left under the hill and were making a rush on us. One more discharge through the embrasure and one to my left were all I had time for before they were on us. I ran to my right, and as I did so the piece next to me was whirled to the left and pointed toward the Yankees, swarming a few feet away from my gun. "Look out, Jim," shouted the gunner, and I fell directly under the muzzle, the discharge passing over me.

The gun was loaded again with a double charge of canister, and Capt. Lumsden ordered, "Fire!" but the primer would not work, and, as the Yankees were almost in arm's reach of us, the captain told us to look out for ourselves. One of the men had another charge of canister in his hand when this order was given, and he threw it into the muzzle of the gun as he turned to run. I learned afterwards that when the Yankees turned it on us it exploded. I had gone about fifty yards down the hill on the jump when I ran over an Enfield rifle that was cocked, the glitter of the cap catching my eye. I snatched it up, turned, and fired at a fellow standing on one of our guns whirling his cap over his head, but did not tarry to see what damage I did. Obliquing to my left, I soon struck the pike and caught up with our infantry, forming behind a stone wall. One of them called to me as I came up: "Say, partner, it was pretty hot over on that hill, wasn't it? You fellows certainly held them back longer than we expected."

After resting awhile, I went to a red brick house, where I found Capt. Lumsden reporting to Gen. Stewart and complaining about being sacrificed. I heard Gen. Stewart say: "Look at the situation, captain; you can see it could not have been helped, but you and your men did all that men could do."

That night I was pouring water from a canteen for Capt. Lumsden to bathe his face and hands. I noticed that he would pick something from his beard, and I asked what it was. "That is poor Rosser's brains, Maxwell," he replied. I learned afterwards that six of our infantry support were killed by one shell, and that an infantry lieutenant and two of his men were killed while helping to handle the first section. They had been forced to seek

protection in our works, as their trench became untenable during the terrific artillery duel and there was nothing they could see to shoot at. But when twelve regiments of Yankee infantry and four regiments of their dismounted cavalry armed with Spencer rifles charged that little squad there was nothing they could do but fire and run, as they couldn't fly. Vision of a Yankee prison added speed to my heels, and nothing but a Yankee bullet could have caught me as I went down the hill.

The [Union] force lined up in our front about 11 a.m. consisted of about fourteen thousand, according to Federal official reports. It was McArthur's Division, of A. J. Smith's Corps, composed of Cogswell's eight-gun

Alexander P. Stewart, C.S.A.

battery. Second Iowa eight-gun battery, and Second Missouri eighteen three-inch rifle guns. The two latter report to have fired one thousand rounds each, and it is presumed Cogswell did the same. Supporting these guns were two lines of battle, twenty paces apart, made up of twelve regiments of infantry. In addition to these, about 1 P.M. Hatch came up with his two brigades of dismounted cavalry and a four-gun battery—amounting in all to 12,457 men and 732 officers, infantry, artillery, and cavalry that were stopped for three hours by Lumsden's little four-gun battery manned by forty-eight officers and men, for our supports could do nothing to assist us.

The truth is, that if the Yankee skirmishers had followed up Ector's skirmishers, who passed us about 11 A.M., we would have been forced to surrender at once and almost without firing a shot. As it was, they spent three hours on us and over three thousand shells, to say nothing of the damage we did them.[36] — CONFEDERATE SERGEANT JAMES R. MAXWELL (Tuscaloosa, Ala.)

DOUGLAS'S BATTERY IN THE BATTLE OF NASHVILLE

☛ Passing over the operations of the first day's battle, on the 15th of December, and night following, I give some personal recollections of the battle and rout of the 16th. Douglas's First Texas Battery, of which I was a private member, was attached at the time to the division of Gen. Edward Johnson, of Lee's Corps, which formed the extreme right of Hood's army, facing Nashville, Douglas's Battery occupied a position west of the Franklin Pike and near the base of a hill, what Gen. Lee calls "Overton Hill."

FORT NEGLEY SITE
The guns of Fort Negley, commanding three turnpikes to the South & Southeast, opened the Battle of Nashville, Dec. 15, 1864. This site was selected by Capt. J. S. Morton as the key strongpoint in the Federal line around the city. The European style fort, named for General James S. Negley, was built of stone, logs, earth & railway iron.

Historical marker at the site of Fort Negley, Nashville, Tenn. (Photo Lochlainn Seabrook)

In common with the other commands on that part of the line, we occupied some temporary earthworks, and were perhaps seventy-five yards in the rear of a stone fence. I distinctly remember the fierce concentrated Federal artillery fire from 9 a.m. to 11 a.m., alluded to by [the report of] Gen. Lee, and the occasional bellowing of the guns of Fort Negley, to which a Northern writer refers. An open space of two and a half miles lay between our lines and those of the Union army, drawn up around the southern suburbs of Nashville, and we could distinctly see their movements.

Following this cannonading two battle lines of two [Union] brigades each—one of white troops, and the other of black—emerged from the Union camps and began to move toward our lines. The negroes were in front. On they came in splendid order, banners flying, mounted officers with drawn swords careering up and down in front of the lines. Then our artillery had its opportunity. All of Lee's guns from the center and wings of his line were turned loose upon the negroes. At first, under the rallying cries and brandishing swords of their white officers, they preserved their alignment in the face of the galling, direct, and enfilading fire of our artillery. Our men were in the white heat and exaltation of battle, and through the brazen throats of their guns poured death and destruction into the ranks of their black foes. Negro nature could stand no more, and, in spite of the domination of their officers, their lines began to waver, and fell back in confusion on the white battle line, some distance in the rear. In due

Edward Johnson, C.S.A.

time their lines were re-formed in the same order, and another attack was attempted, only to be rolled back as before.

In the meantime the Federal forces were making a terrific onslaught on Hood's extreme left, west of our position, and, with their vastly greater numbers, continually overlapping and seeking to turn that flank of our army. Emboldened by the progress of the assault on our left, the attack was renewed about 4 P.M., on Lee's front. In spite of the destructive work of our artillery—the infantry, under orders, reserving their fire—the black and white lines in our front came inexorably forward. Closer and closer they came.

We began to give them double-shotted loads of canister direct in their faces, and our infantry turned loose its fire. The demons of war were reveling in the high carnival of battle. The enemy had reached and were beginning to leap the stone fence in our front. Just at this juncture somebody shouted, "Look to the west!" and, turning in that direction, we saw that the old fields far to the southwest were covered with a mass of Confederate soldiers fleeing diagonally across our rear, in the direction of the Franklin Pike, the only way open to retreat. With lightning like celerity, under orders from Capt. Douglas, our battery horses were brought forward, and we succeeded in escaping with only the loss of two of our artillery pieces. The brave soldiers of our left wing had not been driven in open conflict, but the overlapping Yankee infantry, supplemented by Wilson's corps of cavalry, had succeeded in turning our position and getting in our rear, so that the only resource left was flight.

We had a close call on our immediate part of the line. The Yankees were right on us and shouting, "Hall! halt!" and peppering us with their small arms; but I know of no loss, either by death or capture, except Edward Johnson, our major general, commanding. He was a short, thickset man in, apparently, later middle life. He failed to reach his horse, and undertook, with the rest of us, to climb the hill on foot, but was soon captured. This was his second imprisonment.

The retreat from all parts of the line converged on the mouth of the Franklin Pike, just south of the hill, where it entered a long lane bordered by stone fences. Here the scene beggars description. The mouth of the lane was choked by great masses of wagons and artillery, the drivers in a frenzy of fright and panic, the infantry overleaping the stone fences and spreading through the fields, and the enemy in hot pursuit. Just in this emergency Gen. Lee rode up and called for volunteers to make a stand to check the pursuit. I remember that he asked if there were any South Carolinians present, and asked them to rally to him, he himself being a South Carolinian.

Capt. Douglas manned a section of the battery from his company, and with the support of a few dozen detached infantry men, went back on the hill under the leadership of Gen. Lee, and, unlimbering his guns, fired a number of shots in the direction of the enemy, who were just under the brow of the hill. This had the desired effect, and sufficed to unchoke the pike and give the army a chance to stretch out in orderly retreat.

Following along in the wake of the army, we were halted late at night a few miles north of Franklin, and we lay down in our wet clothes on the soaked earth for such rest as we could get. In the midst of fitful slumber we were aroused in the middle of night by another downpour of freezing rain.[37]
— CONFEDERATE PRIVATE ED W. SMITH (Tyler, Tex.)

JACKSON'S BRIGADE IN THE BATTLE OF NASHVILLE
☛ There are no doubt many survivors of Hood's army who remember that forty-four years ago, on December 16, 1864, we met with disastrous defeat in front of Nashville, Tenn.

Gen. Henry Rootes Jackson's Georgia Brigade, Bate's Division, Cheatham's Corps (of which I was a member), was part of the force which met disaster. I give a short sketch of the movements of the brigade from our discomfiture in front of Murfreesboro, Tenn., to the one in front of Nashville.

After the battle of Franklin, Bate's Division was sent to cooperate with General Forrest in an attack on the garrison at Murfreesboro, which resulted in failure. On account of some dissatisfaction caused by a speech of General Bate, the day after the attack Jackson's Brigade was ordered to report to General Hood at Nashville. Our march to that point was without incident

William B. Bate, C.S.A.

except that we halted long enough at the Tennessee Insane Asylum to cut and haul eight or ten cords of firewood for the inmates of that institution, the superintendent having reported to General Jackson that they were without anything to make fires or to haul wood.

When we arrived at Nashville, Cheatham's Corps was on the extreme right of the Confederate line, the right of which rested on a deep cut on the railroad between Nashville and Murfreesboro. Our brigade was assigned a position about a quarter of a mile in the rear of the line and about half a mile from the railroad, a small hill hiding our camp from the road. This position we occupied for several days, on one of which Brig. Gen. Henry R. Jackson, our brigade commander, had a narrow escape from death. He and several other generals, their staffs and escorts, had assembled on the top of a knoll just in front of Fort Negley on the enemy's fortifications. The group were viewing General Thomas's works and presented a very enticing target for the guns of Fort Negley, which the gunners took advantage of, and one of the shells fired struck the ground under General Jackson's horse, exploding as it struck and killing the horse without injury to the rider. Of course the group quickly sought a safer position.

More Confederate heroes. From left to right: Robert E. Lee, Joseph E. Johnston, Jefferson Davis, Stonewall Jackson, Pierre G. T. Beauregard.

A day or two after this event the enemy commenced massing artillery in front of Cheatham's Corps, which still occupied its position on the right. The initiated at once predicted an assault on that part of the line, and began to prepare to meet it; but just as the batteries commenced firing, a body of troops was observed on our right moving in the direction of the rear of our position. When first seen the distance was too great to tell whether they were white or black; but half an hour later it was known to be a division of negro troops. Every man was on the alert, as this was the first time our corps was to come in contact with [Union] negro soldiers. Seeing that their route of march would bring them across the railroad below the end of the cut, it was decided to make a trap for them, and they were allowed to come on unmolested. After crossing the railroad the darkies formed a line of battle, and, thinking they had not been discovered, prepared to surprise the men in our works by an attack in the rear. Poor fools! little did they dream that every step they took toward the breastworks was watched by angry eyes and twitching fingers on gun triggers, men only awaiting the signal to exterminate them. . . . We took no prisoners. Not a single white man was seen among the killed. Where were their officers?

About the 14th of December our division was moved (the other brigades having joined ours) to the center between the Franklin and Granny White Pikes. We remained in this position one day and part of a night. Our entire corps was then placed on the left of the Granny White Pike, Bate's Division on the right of the corps, Jackson's Brigade on the right of the division, his right resting on the Granny White Pike, and Gen. Edward Johnson's Division across the pike on our right behind a stone fence as breastworks. Finley's Brigade was on our left, with a small hill between us.

On the morning of the 16th, being in need of some blank reports, which were in the headquarters' ambulance, I was going to obtain them when I noticed artillery being massed in front of General Johnson's position. I had just started to return from the ambulance when fire was opened on Johnson's Division, many of the shells passing to the rear and exploding in and about the ambulance. Our driver, named Sigmund, went to the top of the hill to witness the fight, when his head was shot off by a shell.

When I reached the front, every vestige of stone that was in the fence in front of Johnson's men had been knocked down, and the line had sought a safer position a little to the rear. The firing had by this time become general along our entire line. The ground in our front was so rough that no assault was made on us, but our pickets had a lively time with the enemy. We had a fine view of the different assaults on our right, but had no idea that the end would be so disastrous.

The wharf at Nashville as it appeared in the 1860s.

About four o'clock in the afternoon, while seated on the edge of the ditch in the rear of our works engaged in conversation with Capt. Alfred Bryant, our assistant adjutant general, and very near to General Jackson, a loud hurrahing was heard in our rear; and turning to see what it meant, we saw a large body of bluecoats, who had broken through our line at the position held by Finley's men. General Jackson at once instructed Captain Bryant to go down the line to the right and order the regimental commanders to move their men out by the right flank, at the same time sending me to the left with the same instructions. I hurried to the 1st Battalion Georgia Sharpshooters, who were on our extreme left, delivered the order to Lieutenant King, who was in command, and hastened to rejoin

General Jackson. Assisted by Lieutenant Colonel Gordon, of my regiment, the General was walking to where his horse had been sent; but the ground was thawing and the walking slow and tedious. At every step our feet became encumbered with two or three pounds of stiff mud. The enemy were trying to cut us off, and, though at some distance, were firing at us and calling out: "Surrender!"

The General was becoming exhausted, and requested the colonel and myself to leave him. Being near the pike, Colonel Gordon told him that he thought we might get away. The General's horse was in the edge of the woods just beyond, and we felt he could reach the animal. I remained with the General, however. After crossing the pike and while getting over the stone fence it rolled from under him and threw him into the ditch beyond. I assisted him out, and persuaded him to pull his heavy boots off, as they were so loaded with mud that he could scarcely walk. He got one off, and was trying to remove the other when we heard the cry: "Surrender, damn you!" Looking up, we saw the muzzles of four guns aimed at us across the fence not more than seventy or eighty yards distant. "They have got us, General," I said, and called out: "We surrender!"

The General commenced to pull on his boot, and I turned his coat collar down to prevent our captors from discovering his rank, as I hoped we might be recaptured. The men—one corporal and three privates—sprang over the fence and came up to where we stood just as General Jackson succeeded in getting his boot on, and in pulling at it his collar assumed its natural position. The

"The way the fighting was done" at Nashville. The main difference was that the Confederates fought against a well-outfitted army four times the size of their own, one with unlimited manpower, resources, and funding.

corporal walked around the General once or twice, then, standing in front of him, said: "You are a general." "That is my rank," was the reply. The corporal, taking off his hat, waved it around his head and cried out: "Captured a general, by God. I will carry you to Nashville myself."

At a command in German from the corporal two men took charge of the General, and with the corporal crossed the fence to the pike and started with him toward the city, leaving me in charge of the other man, who in very strong language informed me that if I tried to run he would shoot my head off. I told him not to worry, I had run as far as I could. Then he started with me toward Nashville.

We were on the edge of the ground over which Johnson's Division had fallen back, and blankets, knapsacks, etc., were scattered very liberally over it. The Dutchman told me to go to a very large knapsack. When reaching it he proceeded to open and examine the contents. In kneeling to open it he let his gun fall into th e hollow of his left arm, the muzzle almost touching my body. The temptation to knock him in the head took hold upon me; and while he was unbuckling the straps to the knapsack I jerked his gun and, whirling it, struck him back of the head. He fell across the knapsack, when I stepped over him and made off in the direction of the Franklin Pike.

"We must get away from here, as the Yankee cavalry are trying to gain the pike."

Just as I entered the woods I met Lieutenant Colonel Gordon with General Jackson's horse. He asked me for General Jackson, and I reported his capture. "Mount his horse," said the Colonel. "We must get away from here, as the Yankee cavalry are trying to gain the pike in our rear." We rode to the Franklin Pike, where we saw demoralization in the extreme. Riding down the pike about a mile, we saw General Hood, with other commanding officers, trying to rally the men, but in vain. I saw one man who had been stopped by General Cheatham dodge beneath the General's horse and continue on his way while the General was trying to rally others.

The Colonel and I crossed the Harpeth River at Franklin after dark that night, and after finding the General's servant, Jim, turned the horse over to him and instructed him to take the other effects and make his way home to Savannah, Ga., if he could get there. The next day we started for the Tennessee River, which we crossed on the 23rd of December, 1864.[38] — CHARLES B. MARTIN (1st Georgia Volunteers, C.S.A.)

SECTION 2

UNION
RECOLLECTIONS

Union army, outer trenches, Nashville, Tenn., December 16, 1864.

Union Recollections

A UNION PERSPECTIVE OF NASHVILLE

☛ [Union Gen. John M.] Schofield's little army reached Nashville in the morning of December 1st, and was merged in the forces which General [George H.] Thomas was assembling there. General [Andrew J.] Smith, after many unforeseen delays, had arrived with his detachments from the Army of the Tennessee, consisting of three divisions, aggregating nearly twelve thousand men. Of these, something over nine thousand men reached Nashville early in the morning of November 30th, and the rest on the next day. The first intention of General Thomas had been to meet Schofield at Brentwood, ten miles in front of Nashville, with these troops, while Schofield marched the ten miles from Franklin to the same point; but he concluded later to make the union at Nashville.

When he received from Schofield and from [James H.] Wilson the reports of Hood's movement of the 28th and 29th, by which the cavalry had been separated from Schofield, and Forrest was reported pushing eastward, he ordered [James B.] Steedman to leave a garrison in Chattanooga and take his other available forces to Cowan, a station near Elk River, on the Nashville and Chattanooga Railway. Steedman reached there on the morning of the 30th and put his troops in position; but in the evening, Thomas, having learned of Hood's attack in force upon Schofield at Franklin, ordered Steedman to hasten to Nashville. The troops were accordingly put upon the railway trains again, and most of them reached their destination safely on the evening of December 1st. One train, being delayed by an accident, did not arrive till the 2nd, and was attacked by Forrest five miles south of Nashville, but the troops made their way through without serious loss, though the train was captured and destroyed. Of the 8,000 men who had been at Chattanooga on the 30th, Steedman brought with him 5,200, consisting of two brigades of colored troops, and a provisional division made up of soldiers belonging to the army with Sherman, but who had arrived at the front too late to rejoin their own regiments.

George H. Thomas, U.S.A.

Most of the troops under General [Robert S.] Granger, in North Alabama, and of those under General [Robert H.] Milroy, at Tullahoma, were ordered to Murfreesboro, where the whole, amounting to about eight thousand men, were placed under command of General [Lovell H.] Rousseau, and remained until after Hood's defeat on December 15th and 16th. The block-house garrison, at the important railroad bridge on the Elk River, was the only considerable detachment left along the line of the Chattanooga Road, between Murfreesboro and Stevenson.

In Nashville, on November 30th, besides Smith's forces, Thomas had about six thousand infantry and artillery, and three thousand cavalry, mostly dismounted. The Chief Quartermaster, General [James L.] Donaldson, had also armed and organized into a division the employees of his and the commissary department, and these were prepared to serve as an addition to the garrison when needed. The new regiments which arrived were gradually assigned to the old divisions, and the additions to the list of Sherman's convalescents and returning men were united to those who had come with Steedman, making, by December 14th, a division of over five thousand men, under command of General [Charles] Cruft.

Accepting Hood's statements of his losses thus far in the campaign, the army which he led against Nashville consisted of about forty-four thousand men of all arms.[39] His means of information were such that he had pretty full knowledge of the concentration Thomas was now effecting, and the motives which induced a march to Nashville are matters of interesting inquiry. [Pierre G. T.] Beauregard, in his preliminary report to the Confederate War Department, said: "It is clear to my mind that after the great loss of life at Franklin, the army was no longer in a condition to make a successful attack on Nashville." Hood's own statement, which would be entitled to the greatest weight if his subsequent writings were not so full of evidence that they are labored apologies for his misfortunes, is that he expected reinforcements from Texas, and that he hoped by intrenching near Nashville he could maintain himself in a defensive attitude till these should arrive; or that he might even take advantage of a reverse to Thomas, if the latter should be beaten in an attack upon his fortified line. The hope of aid from Texas was a forlorn one, for no organized body of Confederates had for a long time succeeded in passing the Mississippi River.

From other sources, however, we learn that the show of confidence and of success was relied upon to induce recruiting in Tennessee, and that the pretended Governor, [Isham G.] Harris, was with Hood, endeavoring to enforce the conscription in that State. This, and the collection of supplies, give an intelligible reason for occupying as much territory as possible, and for an appearance of bravado which could hardly be justified on military grounds. Doubtless, too, Hood believed that while his veterans might be forced to retreat, they could not be routed; and he underestimated the discouragement that began to pervade them when they were taught, by the terrible lesson of Franklin, how hopeless was that dream of conquest with which their leaders had tried to inspire them when they crossed the

Tennessee [River]. Hood also says he learned that Schofield retreated in alarm; but never was a greater mistake. Schofield's officers on the line had reported their perfect confidence in their ability to hold it, and the withdrawal from the Harpeth had been based solely on the probability of the position being turned before reinforcements could be sure to arrive.

In truth, Hood's situation was a very difficult one, and to go forward or to go back was almost equally unpromising. He followed his natural bent, therefore, which always favored the appearance, at least, of aggression, and he marched after Schofield to Nashville. On approaching the town, he put Lee's corps in the centre, across the Franklin turnpike, for it had suffered least in the campaign, and was now his strongest corps. Cheatham took the right, and Stewart the left of the line, while Forrest, with the cavalry, occupied the country between Stewart and the river below Nashville. Attempts were made to repair the railway from Corinth to Decatur, and thence by Pulaski to Hood's rear. Hood tells us that he gained possession of two locomotives and several cars (perhaps at Spring Hill), and that these were used to help transport supplies.

John M. Schofield, U.S.A.

Thomas put his troops in position upon the heights surrounding Nashville, General Smith's divisions on the right, the Fourth Corps (General Wood temporarily commanding) in the centre, and Schofield's Twenty-third Corps on the left. Steedman, who arrived later, was first put on the Nolansville pike, about a mile in front of Schofield's left, but was placed on the extension of Schofield's line a day or two later, when Wilson, with the cavalry, were sent over the river to Edgefield, on the north bank.

On December 2nd, Hood sent [William B.] Bate's division of Cheatham's corps to destroy the railroad between Nashville and Murfreesboro. Bate reached Overall's Creek, ten miles from Murfreesboro, and attacked the block-house protecting the railway bridge there; but the little garrison held out against a severe cannonade till General Milroy arrived with reinforcements from Murfreesboro, and drove the enemy off. Bate now took the road toward Nashville, and at Stewart's Creek and two other places in that neighborhood, found the block-houses evacuated, and burned them with the bridges they were built to protect. He also reported that he had torn up several miles of track.

Forrest, meanwhile, who had been directed to co-operate with Bate, had sent Buford's division against the block-houses nearest Nashville, and succeeded in reducing three of them near Mill Creek, beginning with one five miles from the city. On the 5th he united Jackson's division with Buford's, and moving toward Lavergne took two more block-houses. He now met Bate, who was moving in the opposite direction, and turned the united forces upon Murfreesboro. Here, on the evening of the 6th, he was further reinforced by Sears's brigade of French's division, and Palmer's brigade of Stevenson's, and on next morning approached the town, reconnoitering the fortifications in person.

Rousseau now sent Milroy against the enemy, with seven regiments, and these attacked vigorously the left flank of Forrest's infantry, while they were moving by his orders in the same direction for the purpose of taking ground farther to the left. Milroy's attack fell obliquely upon the extremity of Bate's line, which was quickly rolled up and put to rout, losing two pieces of artillery. Bate admits 213 casualties in the infantry, but those of the cavalry are not given. Milroy took 207 prisoners, and his own losses in the affair were 30 killed, and 175 wounded. Meanwhile, Buford's division attempted to enter the town by another road, but was also defeated and driven off.

Lovell H. Rousseau, U.S.A.

Bate's division was now recalled to Nashville, and replaced by a brigade under Colonel Olmstead (formerly Mercer's) so that Forrest retained three brigades of infantry as a support for his cavalry. He continued till the 15th to operate on the east of Nashville, and along the south bank of the Cumberland, part of his duty being to "drain the country of persons liable to military service, animals suitable for army purposes, and subsistence supplies." On the 15th Jackson's division captured a railway train of supplies going from Stevenson to Murfreesboro, for the garrison there, who, it would seem, must have been in danger of running short of rations, since the breaking of their communications with Nashville.

At Thomas's request, Lieutenant-Commander Fitch patrolled the Cumberland with gunboats above and below Nashville, to prevent the crossing of that stream by the enemy, and Wilson sent Hammond's brigade of cavalry to Gallatin to watch the north bank of the river as far as Carthage.

From the time of Hood's arrival in front of Nashville, the President [Lincoln] and Secretary of War [Stanton] became very urgent in their desire that Thomas should at once assume the aggressive. At their suggestion, General Grant telegraphed on December 2, advising Thomas to leave the defences of Nashville to General Donaldson's organized employees, and attack Hood at once. Grant's language was scarcely less imperative than an order, but Thomas was so desirous of increasing his force of mounted men that he determined to wait a few days.

On the 8th, the weather, which had been good for more than a week, suddenly changed. A freezing storm of snow and sleet covered the ground, and for two or three days the alternations of rain and frost made the hills about Nashville slopes of slippery ice, on which movement was impracticable. As Hood's positions could only be reached by deployed lines advancing over these hills and hollows, everybody in Thomas's army felt the absolute necessity of now waiting a little longer, till the ice should thaw. This was not fully appreciated by the authorities at Washington, who connected it too closely with Thomas's previous wish for more time, and a rapid correspondence by telegraph took place, in which Thomas was ordered to attack at once or to turn over his command to General Schofield. He assembled his corps commanders and asked their advice, saying that he was ordered to give Hood battle immediately or surrender his command. To whom the army would be transferred was not stated, but it was matter of inference, and he declined to submit the despatch itself to the council of war, though one of the junior officers intimated a wish to know its terms. By the custom of such councils the opinion of officers is given in the inverse order of their grade; but General Schofield, feeling the delicacy of his position as senior subordinate, volunteered his own opinion first, that till the ice should melt it was not now practicable to move.

All concurred in this, and Thomas telegraphed Grant that he felt compelled to wait till the storm should break, but would submit without a murmur if it was thought necessary to relieve him. On the 13th, General [John A.] Logan, who, it will be remembered, was temporarily absent from the Fifteenth Corps, was ordered to Nashville for the purpose of superseding Thomas in command of the Department and Army of the Cumberland, and Grant himself was on the way there also, when the result of the first day of the battle of Nashville (December 15th) stopped further action in that direction.

As early as December 6th, the troops had been ordered to be ready to move against the enemy, and the plan of battle afterward adopted had been in substance determined. From day to day Hood appeared to be taking ground to the east, so as to bring himself more closely into support of Forrest's operations. This led to a suggestion to Thomas from his corps commanders to modify his plan which had looked to

John A. Logan, U.S.A.

the use of the Twenty-third Corps to demonstrate on the left, and give more weight to an attack by the right. From the 8th to the 14[th,] it was definitely understood in camp that an attack would be made the moment the ice melted, and on the date last mentioned a warm rain made it certain the ground would be bare next day. The position of Hood had not materially changed for a week. Chalmers was operating with a division of cavalry along the Cumberland, for some miles below Nashville, as Buford was above; but, while ordinary steamboat transportation was thus interrupted, the navy patrolled the river and prevented the enemy from crossing. Hood had sent a detachment of cavalry

Abraham Buford, C.S.A.

also, supported by Cockrell's brigade of infantry to the mouth of Duck River, on the Tennessee, to blockade that stream also, if possible. In his anxiety to cover so large a territory, the Confederate general was too much extended, and in front of Thomas's right his flank was only covered by Chalmers's division of horse. To make some connection with the river on this side, he had built a number of detached works, but these were not completed, though he had put artillery in them, supported by detachments of infantry from Walthall's division. Reports brought in by deserters indicated that he was intending to withdraw from his advanced lines since the 10th, but the same causes which prevented Thomas from moving, affected him also, and a change of quarters, to his ill-clad and poorly shod troops, would have been the cause of much suffering, if it were made during the severe weather of that week.

On the morning of the 15th a heavy fog obscured the dawn and hid the early movements of Thomas's army. The ice had given place to mud, and the manoeuvres, like those of all winter campaigns, were slow. The modified order of the day directed a strong demonstration by Steedman on the extreme left, with two brigades; one commanded by Colonel Grosvenor, Eighteenth Ohio, and the other (colored troops) commanded by Colonel Morgan, Fourteenth United States Colored. General Wood, with the Fourth Corps, and General Smith, with the Sixteenth Corps, were ordered to form upon a position nearly continuous with the eastern line of the city defences, extending from a salient on the Acklen place across the Hillsborough turnpike toward the Hardin turnpike in a southwest direction. Advancing toward the southeast these corps would make the principal attack obliquely upon the left of Hood's line. General Wilson, with three divisions of cavalry, was ordered to clear the Hardin and Charlotte turnpikes of the enemy (still farther to the west) and move forward on the right of Smith's corps. General Schofield, with the Twenty-third Corps, constituted the reserve, and was placed in rear of Wood, to strengthen and extend the attack on the right. As Smith had occupied the fortifications on the right of the line about the city, these orders would be executed by wheeling the whole of both corps forward to the left, upon the salient at the Acklen place as a pivot, after Wood had taken ground to the right by the distance of say half a mile, so as to bring his left flank at the point named. Schofield, who had been in the fortifications still to the left of Wood, marched from his lines at daybreak, and passing through the works at the Hillsborough pike moved to the east into the position assigned him, as soon as the wheel of the right wing made room for him. The interior lines at the city were held by General Donaldson's men, while General Cruft, with his division, occupied those from which Schofield and Steedman moved.

Standing in the salient in Wood's line, which has been mentioned, the topography of the country about Nashville is clearly seen. On the left, toward the east, is a valley in which Brown's Creek flows north into the Cumberland. It rises in the high Brentwood Hills, which shut out the view toward the south a little more than four miles away, and its course is nearly parallel to the eastern line of Thomas's intrenchments. On the right, but a little farther off, is Richland Creek, flowing northwest into the Cumberland. It rises also in the Brentwood Hills, not more than a mile west of Brown's Creek, and runs nearly parallel with it toward the city for some distance, when the two curve away to right and left, encircling the place, and marking its strong and natural line of defence. On the high ridge between the creeks is the Granny White turnpike. A mile eastward is the Franklin turnpike, diverging about thirty degrees. At nearly equal distances, on that side, the Nolensville and Murfreesboro turnpikes leave the city successively. Turning toward the west from our station, the Hillsboro, the Hardin, and the Charlotte turnpikes successively go out at similar angles, all radiating from the centre of the town. The ground is hilly, rising into knobs and eminences two or three hundred feet above the Cumberland, but mostly open, with groves of timber here and there.

Hood's line was over Brown's Creek, on the high ground from the Nolensville turnpike and the Chattanooga railway to the Franklin turnpike, then crossing the creek and mounting a high hill west of it, it extended to the Hillsboro road, where it turned back along a stone wall on the side of the turnpike. The detached works, of which mention has been made, were still to the southwest of this, and across Richland Creek. The relative places of his several corps were the same as when he first came before the town. His main line at his left, where it reached the Hillsboro pike, was about a mile in front of Wood, but he also occupied an advanced line with skirmishers, only half that distance away, and terminating in a strong outpost on Montgomery Hill, at the Hillsboro road.

Before six o'clock in the morning Steedman was moving forward under cover of the fog by the Murfreesboro road, on the extreme left, and about eight he attacked Hood's right between the turnpike and the railway. The vigor of the assault made it something more than a demonstration, and the rapid fire of both artillery and small arms attracted the attention of the enemy in that direction. The distance Smith's right wing had to move was found to be greater than had been reckoned on, and it was ten o'clock before McArthur's division had moved sufficiently to the left to open the way for Wilson's cavalry to advance upon the Hardin road.

Johnson's division moved forward on the Charlotte turnpike, looking also after the enemy's battery at Bell's Landing, on the Cumberland; Croxton's brigade took the interval to the Hardin turnpike, Hatch's division continued the line to the flank of Smith's infantry, and Knipe's division was in reserve. Smith formed the Sixteenth Corps with Garrard's division on his left, connecting with the Fourth Corps, and McArthur's division on the right. The division of Moore was in reserve.

On the other side Chalmers did what he could to oppose them, supported by Coleman's (formerly Ector's) brigade of infantry, but the odds was too great, and they were driven steadily back. Half a mile southeast of the Hardin road the first of Hood's detached works, containing four guns, was found. The batteries of McArthur and Hatch were brought to bear upon it from all sides, and, after a severe cannonade, McMillan's and Hubbard's brigades of infantry and Coon's of cavalry (dismounted) attacked and carried the redoubt. Stewart now recalled Coleman and directed him to report to Walthall, whose division occupied the stone wall bordering the Hillsboro turnpike. Walthall placed him on the extension of his line southward, upon some

Nashville has changed drastically in appearance and size since the battle that raged here in December 1864.

high points covering the Granny White road. This left the other redoubts to their fate, as Chalmers was far too much over-matched to make much resistance with his cavalry. He had been driven back so fast that his train, with his headquarters baggage and papers, had been captured. The next redoubt, about four hundred yards to the right, was carried by the same troops, and two guns in it were taken. Another four-gun battery, intrenched on a detached hill, was stormed and captured by the cavalry, and a two-gun battery by Hill's brigade of McArthur's division, though with the loss of Colonel Hill, who fell in the moment of success. Smith's corps now bore somewhat to the left, striking the extreme flank of the stone wall held by Walthall's division, driving Reynolds's brigade from it in confusion. At the same time, Schofield, who had followed the movement closely with the Twenty-third Corps, in accordance with Thomas's order, pushed Couch's division (formerly Cooper's) past Smith's flank, and beyond the last redoubt which had been captured. Now advancing on the line from the Hillsboro road, eastward, across an open valley half a mile wide, Couch assaulted and carried the left of a series of hills parallel to the Granny White turnpike. The assault was made by Cooper's brigade, and the rest of the division was quickly brought up in support, while Cox's division marched still farther to the right and occupied the continuation of the line of hills along Richland Creek with two brigades, keeping the third (Stiles's) on the heights west of the creek to cover the flank.

These last movements had occurred just as darkness was falling, and completed the day's work on the extreme right. It is now necessary to go back and trace the progress of the Fourth Corps. General Wood had formed the corps with Elliott's division (formerly Wagner's) on the right, connecting with Smith's corps, while Kimball's and Beatty's extended the line to the left. The time occupied in the deployed movement of the right of the army made it one o'clock before it was time for the extreme left to move. Wood then ordered forward Post's brigade of Beatty's division to attack Montgomery Hill, the high point half a mile in front of the salient of our line, on which was Hood's advanced guard.

The assault was preceded by rapid artillery fire and was gallantly executed. The general advance of the line was now progressing, and Schofield's corps was ordered away by General Thomas to support the movement of the right flank. Wood met with a strong skirmishing resistance, but the lines went forward steadily, keeping pace with the troops on the right, till Smith's attack upon the south end of the stone wall along the Hillsboro road, which was held by Walthall. Kimball's division was opposite the angle in Hood's line where Walthall joined upon Loving, having Sears's brigade of French's division between them. Kimball pushed straight at the angle, and the right of the stone wall having already been carried, Walthall's brigades, under Johnston (formerly Quarles's) and Shelley, successively gave way. Elliott's division of Wood's corps lapped upon Garrard's of the Sixteenth, and the whole went forward with enthusiasm, capturing several guns and many prisoners.

Hood's left was now hopelessly broken, and he made haste to draw back his shattered divisions upon a new line. Schofield's advance had separated Coleman's brigade from Walthall, but it occupied a commanding hill (afterward known as Shy's Hill), and held on with tenacity till Walthall, helped by the gathering darkness, could form along its right across the

Granny White road. At the first news of the loss of the redoubts, Hood ordered Cheatham's corps (except Smith's, formerly Cleburne's division) from the right to the left, and his divisions, hurrying by the Franklin pike toward Overton's Hill, passed great numbers of stragglers streaming to the rear. Bate was ordered to relieve part of Walthall's division, so as to make a stronger line between Shy's Hill and the Granny White road, and Walthall closed to the right upon Loring. South of Shy's Hill, Lowry's (formerly Brown's) division extended the Confederate left in front of Schofield, and the whole worked diligently to intrench themselves. Lee's corps was drawn back till his right encircled Overton's Hill, on which Clayton's division was placed, supported by Brantley's brigade, while Stevenson's and Johnson's divisions extended the line to the west till it united with Loring's division of Stewart's corps.

"The assault was preceded by rapid artillery fire and was gallantly executed."

On our left Steedman had kept his men active. He had attacked and carried an earthwork near the Raines house early in the day, and had followed up the progressive movement of the army, harassing the enemy's right as it drew back.

About nightfall there was a strong appearance of a precipitate retreat of the enemy, and Thomas ordered Wood to move his corps farther to the left, reaching the Franklin turnpike, if possible, and to push southward upon it. This direction was a wise one if the enemy continued his retreat, for it prevented the crowding of the army upon a single road; but had Thomas been sure that Hood would reform upon the new line, he would, no doubt, have continued the general movement of the day by extending his forces to the right. The darkness stopped Wood before he had reached the Franklin road, and he bivouacked where night overtook him, ready to continue the march in the morning. His right was near Smith's left, and his own left was diagonally toward the rear, in the works which Lee's corps had abandoned on the hither side of Brown's Creek.

For the results obtained, the losses had been astonishingly light. Wood reports only three hundred and fifty casualties in his corps, Smith's were about the same, and Schofield's not over one hundred and fifty. Those of Steedman and of Wilson were proportionately small, though the exact figures cannot be given, as the losses of the first and second days are not discriminated in any report but Wood's. Sixteen pieces of artillery and twelve hundred prisoners had been taken, and Hood's whole line had been driven back fully two miles. The work was not completed, but should the enemy maintain his position, the promise for the morrow was good.

Hood now realized the mistake his over-confidence had led him into, by inducing him not only to extend his lines beyond what was prudent, but, worst of all, to allow Forrest to become so far detached that he could not be recalled in time for the battle.[40] Sears's brigade had been brought back to the lines before the 15th, but two others were still with Forrest, and Cockrell's was at Duck River.

The Confederate commander set to work in earnest, however, to repair his mistake. The cavalry was too far away to join him in twenty-four hours, but orders were despatched recalling Forrest, and preparations were made to hold the new line another day. As his left still seemed his weak point, Hood ordered the whole of Cheatham's corps to that flank. Shy's Hill, which was held by Coleman's brigade, made the angle in the line, from which the sharply refused flank continued southward, Lowry's division and Smith's (formerly Cleburne's) extending it to the Brentwood Hills. Bate's division was placed, as we have already seen, between Shy's Hill and the flank of Stewart's corps, facing north. Chalmers's division of cavalry was close upon the left of the infantry, bending the line back, somewhat, toward the Granny White road.

The Confederate line now rested upon high hills, Overton's and Shy's, between which the ground was lower, though rolling, and was broken by the upper branches of Brown's Creek, which ran in nearly straight courses northward, crossing Hood's position at right angles. Overton's hill was a broad, rounded elevation, and the works, in curving southward around its summit, did not present any sharp angle to weaken their strength. Shy's Hill, however, though high, was of less extent, and the lines of Bate and Lowry made a right angle there. Bate complained of the position, but Hood's engineers had established it, and Cheatham did not feel at liberty to change it. Indeed, it could not have been changed much, unless the whole Confederate army were to retreat. Coleman had been driven to Shy's Hill by Schofield's advance at dusk, and had all he could do to hold on to it at all. The extension of the Twenty-third Corps along the east side of Richland Creek left only the hills directly south of Shy's unoccupied, and it was there alone that the advance of Thomas's right wing could be checked.

The National skirmish lines were so close that the digging had to be done on the inside of the parapet chiefly, getting cover for the men as soon as possible. The hill on our side, held by Couch's division, was only three hundred yards from Shy's, and the work on the latter, built under fire, was weak. Farther south, the confronting hills, held by the rest of Cheatham's corps on the one side, and Schofield's on the other, were farther apart, and that in the Confederate line was considerably higher and well wooded on the top. A strong work was made upon it, revetted with timber, with embrasures for cannon, and a parapet high enough to defilade the interior; but the fire of our sharpshooters prevented any abatis being made.

General Thomas held a council with his corps commanders in the evening, but no new orders seem to have been issued, except some directions as to movements in the event of a retreat of Hood during the night. If he remained in position, the movements progressing at the close of the day would be continued. During the night the lines on the National [Union] side also were adjusted. In Schofield's corps, Couch's division, in making connection with Smith, opened a gap between it and Cox's division, which, after extending the two brigades, which

George H. Thomas, U.S.A.

were over Richland Creek, in single line, without reserves, was still unable to join Couch's left by as much as three hundred yards. The disadvantage of drawing in and contracting the extension of the right flank was so manifest, that, upon the report of the fact, Schofield applied to Smith for some of his reserves to complete the line, and at six o'clock in the morning, Colonel Moore reported with five regiments and a battery, and was placed there. Three of the regiments were put in the trenches already there, and two in support of the artillery in rear.

At the same hour, Wood resumed the movement of the Fourth Corps, which had been interrupted in the evening, and Steedman advanced upon the Nolensville pike to the abandoned line of the Confederate works, where he half wheeled to the right and came up on Wood's left. The latter first formed his corps with Beatty's division on the left of the Franklin road, and Kimball's on the right, with Elliott in reserve; but finding a large space vacant between himself and the centre of the army, he moved Elliott's division forward into line continuous with Smith's corps. The left of the Fourth Corps, where it now connected with Steedman, remained across the Franklin road, and opposite Overton's Hill, where Hood's line bent back to the south. The National [Union] line, therefore, instead of being oblique to the enemy, and far outreaching it on the right, as on the previous day, was parallel and exterior to it from flank to flank, nowhere reaching beyond it, except where Wilson's cavalry was operating beyond Schofield on the Hillsboro road.

About noon, Steedman's troops formed a connection with Wood's, and the latter, by order of General Thomas, took direction of both. Along the whole line the skirmishers were advanced close to the enemy's works, and various points were reconnoitered to determine the feasibility of an assault. Thomas did not order an attack upon the [Confederate] intrenchments, but left the corps commanders to their own discretion in this respect. Wood concentrated his artillery fire upon Overton's Hill, Smith and Schofield maintained a severe cross-fire upon the [Confederate] angle at Shy's Hill, and at other points on the line the opposing batteries were warmly engaged.

Finding that the enemy was strongly intrenched in Wood's front, General Thomas rode to Smith, and learned the results of the reconnaissance there, and, after examining for himself the position, continued on to Schofield's lines on the right. Schofield had ordered Stiles's brigade of Cox's [the writer of this article] division to leave its position in rear of the extreme right and march farther south, then, turning to the east, to push forward upon a wooded hill on the extension of the line of the division. Thence he was to keep pace with the advance of Wilson's dismounted cavalry, and attack with the rest of the line when it should go forward. The termination of the Confederate continuous works in Cheatham's line, was the embrasured earthwork already referred to, with a recurved flank facing the south. A four-gun battery, of smooth twelve-pound guns, was in this fort, with four more in the curtain connecting it with Shy's Hill. The rifled guns of Cockerell's battery, on the west side of Richland Creek, were able to reach the embrasures of the work in front, while the shells of the smooth guns fell short in the efforts at reply, and the superiority of the National artillery was such that the Confederate gunners were forced to reload their pieces, by drawing them aside with the *prolonge*, to the protection of the parapet.

On learning the nature of the works in front of Schofield, and the extent of the enemy's line, Thomas ordered Smith to send one of his divisions to extend that flank, but on representations as to the condition of affairs in Smith's front, the order was withdrawn.

Wilson, however, was making good progress with his cavalry, which must now be traced. Johnson's division had not felt strong enough to attack the position of Chalmers, near Bell's Landing, on the 15th, and Wilson's movements had been made with the rest of the corps. The concentration of Chalmers's division in the night, enabled Wilson to bring Johnson up in the morning, and he now had all three of his divisions in hand. Hammond's had pickets toward the Granny White turnpike, in rear of Hood's left, Hatch's division was ordered to move from his bivouac on the Hillsboro road, on the left of Hammond, and upon the enemy's rear. Johnson was moving across the country from near Bell's Landing. By noon, or shortly after, Wilson's skirmishers formed a continuous curved line from Schofield's right around the enemy's flank across the Granny White road. It was at this time that Schofield ordered the movement of Stiles's brigade, which has been mentioned, and had suggested the desirability of sending a full division of infantry beyond Hood's flank, if one could be spared from the line. He did not think it wise to assault the heavy work in front of Cox's division, except in connection with a general advance.

The situation at the angle on Shy's Hill, however, was opening the prospect of a successful attack there. The advance of Wilson's dismounted cavalry from one wooded hill to another on the south, was making Hood uneasy, and his vehement exhortation to Chalmers, to hold his own, not being enough to overcome the odds against that officer, he was forced to withdraw Govan's brigade from Cheatham's line, and send it to Chalmers's support. Bate was ordered to extend his left, and occupy Shy's Hill, while Coleman, who had been there, was sent to fill Govan's place. Bate's line was now a good deal stretched, and he found also that the earthworks built in the night were too far back from the brow of the hill, so that they did not command its slope. The fire upon it was too hot to change it, he could get no reinforcements, and he could only hold on to the last.

[In his official report] Bate's own words best describe his situation in the afternoon: "The enemy," he says, "opened a most terrific fire of artillery, and kept it up during the day. In the afternoon, he planted a battery in the woods, in the rear of Mrs. Bradford's house (this was in McArthur's line), fired directly across both lines composing the angle, and threw shells directly in the back of my left brigade; also placed a battery on a hill diagonally to my left, which took my first brigade in reverse. (This was in Cox's line.) The batteries on the hill, in its front, not more than three hundred yards distant (in Couch's line) had borne the concentrated fire of my Whitworth rifles all day, and must have suffered heavily, but were not silenced. These rifled guns of the enemy being so close, razed the works on the left of the angle for fifty or sixty yards."

General McArthur, from his position, was able to see something of the mischief done to Bate's line, and reported that an assault upon the angle was practicable. He proposed to move McMillan's brigade to the right, in front of the hill held by Couch, and to charge under the cover of Couch's guns, where the hillside gave most protection to an advance. Thomas approved the plan, and Smith sent to Schofield for directions to Couch to co-operate. Schofield acceded to this, and directed Cox also to attack the hill in his front simultaneously, while Stiles should advance beyond the flank with the cavalry. It was now near four o'clock, and Thomas was in person at Schofield's position, from which Shy's Hill, and the whole range south, to the Brentwood Hills, were in full view.

The whole connection of events will be best understood if we now return to the left flank, where Wood had been making anxious examination

John McArthur, U.S.A.

of the enemy's position on Overton's Hill, and upon the report of a reconnaissance by Colonel Post, had determined to try the chances of an attack there. The assault from the Fourth Corps' position was assigned to Post's brigade of Beatty's division, supported by Streight's. Thompson's colored brigade, of Steedman's command, supported by Grosvenor's brigade, were to attack at the same time from the east. A concentrated artillery fire upon the hill preceded the assault, and at three o'clock the order to advance was given.

A cloud of skirmishers ran forward to draw the enemy's fire and to annoy the artillerists in the works, and the brigades in line followed them. Nearing the

William M. Shy, C.S.A.

intrenchments, they rushed forward, some of the men gaining the parapet, but they were received with so hot a fire, that they could not endure it, and after a short, sharp struggle they recoiled. Their retreat was covered by the rest of Beatty's division and Steedman's reserves, and by the artillery. These were so handled that the enemy did not venture from his works, and our wounded were brought safely off; but the casualties were probably half of all that occurred in the battle, adding another to the many proofs of the terrible disadvantage at which a direct assault of a well intrenched line is usually made. Colonel Post was killed, and the loss in officers was heavy, for they exposed themselves fearlessly in leading their men.

At the angle in the Confederate works held by Bate, at Shy's Hill, the circumstances were different. His lines, as we have seen, were enfiladed and taken in reverse; his parapet was levelled for some distance; the closeness of Couch's batteries, the near approach of our skirmishers, the attenuation of Bate's troops, the cover for the approach of the assailing force under the hill-slope, all combined to neutralize the advantage of modern weapons, and to give the assault the preponderance of chances which justify it. While the fire upon the angle was kept up with increasing severity, McArthur ordered Colonel McMillan to form his brigade in the hollow before Couch's works, and when they should be half-way up the hill, the brigades to the left were to advance in *echelon*, attacking the lower line before them.

Wilson's dismounted cavalry had been advancing from the south, gaining position after position, and increasing their ardor as they advanced. Their numbers enabled them to outflank Govan's brigade, which Hood had sent to assist Chalmers in holding them back, and as they approached

Schofield's position Stiles's brigade of infantry came in close support. The balls from this attacking force were now falling in rear of Bate and Lowry, and the men of Cleburne's old division were vainly trying to form a line long or strong enough to match that which was coming from the south. Wilson had gone in person to Thomas, at Schofield's position, to report what his men were doing, and reached him just as McMillan's brigade was seen to rush forward upon the slope of Shy's Hill. At a sign from Schofield, Cox's division started also on the run, Doolittle's brigade in advance. Wilson turned to gallop back to his command, but before he could get half-way there, the whole Confederate left was crushed in like an egg-shell.

McMillan swept unchecked over Bate's ruined line at Shy's Hill. The gallant Colonel [William M. Shy] of the Thirty-seventh Georgia did all that man could do to hold it, and dying at his post, gave to the height the name it bears. The arch was broken; there were no reserves to restore it, and from right and left the Confederate troops peeled away from the works in wild confusion. From the heavy earthwork in front of Doolittle one volley of cannon and small arms was fired, but in the excitement it was aimed so high as to do no mischief, and Cox's whole division was over the works

Jacob D. Cox, U.S.A.

before they could reload. At the same time Hatch and Knipe, with their divisions of dismounted men, rushed in from the right, and, abandoning their artillery, the Confederates west of the Granny White road crowded eastward, running for life. Some were killed, many were captured, and Smith's and Schofield's men met upon the turnpike at right angles, and were halted to prevent their organizations from being confused together.

Hubbard's brigade, of McArthur's division, which followed McMillan's movement, met with more resistance, and suffered more severely; but though some of the Confederate regiments held tenaciously to their works, and surrendered in form, most of the troops broke their organizations entirely when the advance was taken up from centre to wings, and Wood's divisions now charged, with hardly a show of opposition, over Overton's Hill, from which they had been driven back an hour before.[41] — UNION GENERAL JACOB DOLSON COX

A BRILLIANT & DECISIVE VICTORY

☛ The morning of December 15 was soft and muddy, not the best sort of day for the evolutions of either infantry or cavalry, but infinitely better than the universal glare of ice that had preceded. The position of the Union army was one of great excellence, whether for attack or for defence.

The city of Nashville, situated in a pocket formed by a great double curve of the Cumberland River, was encompassed in front by low hills, upon which a strong line of intrenchments with occasional redoubts had been built all the way from the river-bank above the city to the river-bank below. This interior defensive line was manned with "quartermaster's forces." In front of this line on the extreme Union left, between the Lebanon turnpike and the Chattanooga railway, was stationed Steedman's division. To the rear and right of Steedman, but within the interior line, was massed the Twenty-third corps, commanded by Schofield, and intended to play the part of a reserve. To the right of Schofield came the Fourth corps, now commanded by the veteran Wood, since Stanley had been wounded in the battle of Franklin.

A salient in Wood's line, where the Hillsboro turnpike crossed Laurens Hill, occupied nearly the centre of the Union battle-front. To the right of Wood came the Sixteenth corps, under Andrew Smith, with its right wing refused and extending beyond the Charlotte turnpike. Both Wood and Smith were strongly intrenched. On the extreme right, between the Charlotte road and the river, was stationed Wilson's fine corps of cavalry. Behind the city the river was patrolled by gunboats. Nearly the entire space occupied by the Federal army was inclosed by two small streams, Richland and Brown's creeks, rising in the Brentwood Hills, four miles south of Nashville, and flowing into the Cumberland River. On the high crest of the Brentwood range stood the humble abode of a venerable dame, after whom the road passing by was known as the Granny White pike. About midway between Granny White's house and the city the space between the forks of Richland and Brown's creeks was occupied by a low and somewhat broken line of hills, which extended northeastward as far as the Chattanooga railway.

James B. Steedman, U.S.A.

Upon this line of hills Hood's army was intrenched. Cheatham's corps was on the extreme right, by the railway; the centre, commanded by Stephen D. Lee, of South Carolina, stretched across the Franklin pike; and on the left Stewart's corps reached to the Hillsboro road, where its left wing was sharply refused. A stone wall, running along the roadside for 1,000 yards or so, was utilized as a screen for rifle-pits, and at three commanding points strong batteries were planted, while about a mile to the southwest, beyond a fork of Richland Creek, two detached hills were crowned with redoubts. A further attempt was made to strengthen the Confederate left by placing a rather solid skirmish line in front of Stewart's corps, terminating in an intrenched position on Montgomery Hill, close to the Hillsboro pike, and not more than half a mile distant from Wood's salient upon Laurens Hill. The situation boded no good to the Confederate army.

These defences of its left wing were but flimsy as compared with the solid masses of Federal infantry and cavalry west of the Hillsboro pike. It was hardly prudent in Hood, under the circumstances, to accept battle. If he had been a Stonewall Jackson, he might have attempted to withdraw stealthily from his position and verify Grant's forebodings by slipping across the Cumberland River and dashing northward. But in presence of the lynx-eyed Thomas even Jackson might have proved unequal to such an exploit.

Nathan B. Forrest, C.S.A.

Perhaps Hood might have fared better had he taken position in the first place back upon the Brentwood Hills. But in any case, with only 38,000 men against Thomas's 55,000, he could hardly look for victory.[42] Clearly the worst thing Hood could do was to diminish the numbers which he could put into the battle, and this mistake he did commit. He kept Forrest, with the greater part of the cavalry and three brigades of infantry, patrolling the country east of Nashville, "to drain it of persons liable to military service, animals suitable for army purposes, and subsistence supplies." When the battle was fought, Forrest was too far astray to be promptly recalled, and Hood's only reliance against the powerful Union cavalry was the division of Chalmers, with which he watched the Charlotte turnpike.

Thomas's plan of battle was to make a left wheel with his whole right wing, pivoting upon Wood's salient at Laurens Hill. At the proper moment Wood might threaten the rebel works on Montgomery Hill, or perhaps attack and carry them, and press on against Stewart's angle. Meanwhile Steedman was to make a vigorous demonstration against Cheatham's right upon the Chattanooga railway, and Schofield's reserve was to play such a part as circumstances might determine.

The early morning of December 15 was foggy, but a hot sun had burned off the vapours before nine o'clock. The movements began at daybreak. Steedman crossed Brown's Creek and began a demonstration that was virtually an assault, and kept Cheatham's corps busy all day. This attack, moreover, neutralized Lee's corps and made it useless; for when the alarming pressure was felt upon Stewart's left, Lee could not substantially reinforce either Stewart or Cheatham without leaving either a gap or a very thin line at the Franklin pike, and this he dared not do lest the garrison of the interior Federal line opposite should sally from its works and, charging straight down the Franklin road, pierce the rebel centre.

Observe, dear reader, the brilliancy of Thomas's tactics. Here at the outset, by employing only Steedman's division and keeping his "quartermaster's forces" in their works, he eliminates Lee and Cheatham, two thirds of the rebel army, from the problem! The serious work before him now is to pulverize Stewart, and for this purpose he can use Wilson, Smith, Wood, and Schofield, nearly his whole force! This has the true Napoleonic flavour; it smacks of Austerlitz.

The grand wheel with the Federal right wing began early, but an hour or more was lost by some of Smith's infantry at first getting in the way of Wilson's cavalry. No serious harm was done, however. Wilson was presently in position on Smith's right, driving Chalmers steadily back. By noon the entire Federal right wing had wheeled past the Hardin pike and across Richland Creek, and formed a line parallel to the Hillsboro pike, extending from the pivot on Laurens Hill southward to the detached hills that were

James H. Wilson, U.S.A.

crowned with rebel redoubts. Thomas wished to prolong this line still further, and therefore ordered out Schofield's corps, which marched behind Wood and Smith until it took position on Smith's right, facing the Hillsboro pike nearly opposite, and about a mile and a half west of Granny White's house. The van of Wilson's cavalry then pushed forward to the Granny White pike.

While these things were going on, Wood sent forward a single brigade, under Colonel Philip Sidney Post, to storm Montgomery Hill. This work was done quickly and well; the hill with its guns was soon in our hands, along with more prisoners than it was convenient to handle.

At about two p.m. the detached redoubts were stormed by some of Smith's infantry and Hatch's division of cavalry dismounted, and their cannon were turned upon the enemy.

Next came Wood's assault in force upon Stewart's angle at the stone wall. By four p.m. all the works here had been carried, and the Confederate left wing was pushed off the ground. Darkness soon stopped the fighting, and the men slept wherever they happened to be.

Stewart's corps had been driven southward two miles, and lay across the Granny White pike. At nightfall Hood withdrew Cheatham's corps from the Nolensville road, and transferred it to his left, facing Schofield. Stewart thus became the centre, and Lee was placed on his right, with wing refused on Overton Hill. It was a stronger position than he had occupied in the morning, but his men were dispirited with the day's work, while Thomas's men, from the major-generals down to the privates, were aglow with the instinct of victory, and felt themselves invincible.

Strong as Hood's position was, its left wing was in danger of being turned by reason of Thomas's superior numbers, especially in his cavalry. On the morning of the 16th Thomas brought his forces close up to the enemy: Steedman on the left by the railway facing southward, Wood next, then Smith standing across the Granny White pike, then Schofield parallel to the Hillsboro pike and facing eastward, finally Wilson's cavalry threatening the enemy's flank. In order to save this flank, it was necessary that it should be sharply refused, and thus a salient was created at Shy Hill,[43] the steep summit of which was fortified as well as haste would permit. Upon this salient Smith and Schofield set up a deadly cross-fire, enfilading the Confederate lines in two directions.

So much time had been consumed in moving the troops into position over the execrably soft and uneven ground that noon was past before heavy fighting began. While Schofield and Smith were hammering at the salient upon Shy Hill, an attack was made upon the Confederate right wing at Overton Hill. Colonel Post, of Wood's corps, who had acquitted himself so nobly the day before, undertook to storm the enemy's intrenchments. He was supported by Thompson's brigade of coloured troops, from Steedman's division. The utmost bravery was shown, by negroes as well as by white men, but the assault met with a bloody repulse. Colonel Post received an ugly wound, and was made brigadier general on the field for his gallantry. His unsuccessful assault was not without its effect upon the result of the battle. It made Hood uneasy about his right wing, so that he took one of Cheatham's divisions—the one formerly commanded by Cleburne—and sent it to reinforce Lee's troops on Overton Hill.

At the same time the pressure of the Union cavalry upon Chalmers grew so alarming that Hood withdrew a brigade of infantry from Cheatham in order to support Chalmers. By these successive depletions Cheatham's line was weakened, and the angle upon Shy Hill became so thin as to invite assault. Thereupon one of Smith's brigades scrambled up the steep slope and with levelled bayonets drove the defenders from their works. At the same time a few pieces of Federal artillery, dragged up to an eminence that commanded Shy Hill, opened fire; while a brigade of Hatch's cavalry rushed along the Granny White road and poured in a quick succession of volleys from their repeating rifles. Just then Thomas hurled forward the extreme right division of Schofield's corps, and in a few minutes the whole Confederate left had become a disorderly mob running wildly for the Franklin turnpike. This was the signal for a grand advance along the whole Federal line. Stewart and Lee were driven back in utter confusion, and Steedman's negroes swept victorious over the hill which an hour before had so sternly repulsed them. Never was rout more complete and final than that of Hood.

The pursuit was kept up for ten days, ending at the Tennessee River below Decatur, on the day after Christmas. The Union loss in killed and wounded, at the battle of Nashville, was about 3,000. The total Union loss in the whole campaign of five weeks was not more than 6,000. In warfare sound strategy and sound tactics are the great economizers of human life. The Confederate loss in killed and wounded cannot be estimated with accuracy; but during

William T. Sherman, U.S.A.

the battle and the pursuit Thomas reported the capture of at least 13,000 prisoners and 72 cannon.[44] The Confederate army in the West was virtually annihilated. Nashville was the most decisive victory gained by either side in the Civil War, and one of the most brilliant.

The destruction of Hood's army enabled Sherman to march northward from Savannah through the Carolinas, and the western situation was so simplified that Schofield's force was transferred from Thomas to Sherman. At the eleventh hour the Confederate government appointed Robert E. Lee its general-in-chief, and Lee appointed Joseph E. Johnston to command such forces as could be scraped together to oppose Sherman. Of these there were about 15,000 men (one third of them being the remnant of the Hood wreckage) to contend against Sherman's 90,000.

At Petersburg and Richmond, Lee, with about 60,000, was confronted by Grant, with 125,000. When Sherman arrived at Raleigh, within 120 miles of Lee, while Stoneman, seizing the railway between Lynchburg and Knoxville, cut off the possibility of retreat from Virginia into the Tennessee Mountains, the Confederacy had evidently reached the last ditch. Lee's position, so long and so skillfully held, had become untenable. The only question was whether he should succumb right there, or, letting go Richmond, should unite his forces with those of Johnston. In the latter case the twain would have been crushed between the two great Union armies as between the upper and the nether millstone.

Should the Confederacy's two foremost heroes be vanquished separately or together? Sheridan's victory at Five Forks cut away the latter alternative,

and virtually ended the aggressive proceedings which began on the spring day in St. Louis when Grant and Sherman congratulated Lyon and Blair upon the capture of Camp Jackson.[45] — JOHN FISKE (Yankee historian; based his article on official Union military reports)

GEN. THOMAS & THE BATTLE OF NASHVILLE

☛ This terrible battle was fought December 15 and 16, 1864, the sequel to that of Franklin, November 30, just fifteen days before. On that night (November 30) the army of Gen. Schofield fell back on Nashville, leaving the Union dead on the battlefield, to be buried by the Confederates. On the morning of December 1, after the Union army had reached Nashville and were comfortably quartered on the tented field, the rain, hail, and snow fell in torrents and continued for some ten days. The surface of the earth was covered with ice. *The Union soldiers were well clad and fed and in comfortable quarters* (reenforcements were being received as rapidly as transportation could bring them to Nashville), while *the Confederate soldiers, encamped just a mile or more from the outskirts of the city, were thinly clad, many without hats or shoes, in poor quarters, short rations, with nothing to burn but green timber*, as every fence rail for miles had been consumed.

The lines of the Confederate troops under Gen. Hood rested on the Cumberland River, above and below Nashville. Gen. George H. Thomas, familiarly known as "Pap" Thomas, commanded the Union forces. His headquarters were in the old St. Cloud Hotel building, corner of Summer and Church Streets. He was master of the situation. Almost hourly he was waited upon by some of the prominent citizens of Nashville, and the question put to him: "Had

The Cumberland River, Nashville, Tenn., as it looks today. (Photo Lochlainn Seabrook)

we not better remove our families out of Nashville to Louisville or elsewhere in the event of the bombardment of the city?" The stereotyped reply was all that fell from the General's lips: "I shall give you due warning when the time arrives."

The General seemed to have the most implicit confidence in winning the battle, if only left to his own judgment when to bring on the attack. The authorities at Washington were hourly ordering him to bring on the engagement, but he heeded not the order. Finally like orders came so thick and fast that he replied to the effect that if the engagement must be brought on before he was ready another commander must be chosen. Gen. John A. Logan was ordered to assume command. Gen. Logan was serving in the East. He knew of the fighting qualities of Gen. Thomas, and was in no haste to reach Nashville. Before his arrival. Gen. Thomas, not governed by orders or telegrams, but alone by the situation and surrounding circumstances, on the early morning of December 15, 1864, moved out on the Granny White Pike, and the great battle was soon commenced, which lasted for two days, and was one of the severest struggles of the war. This battle was said to have "crushed the backbone of the rebellion." This expression was used by Gov. [William G.] Brownlow after the war when presenting a gold medal to Gen. Thomas, awarded by the State Legislature. The Governor, in the presentation, said: "I give this medal to the general who won the first Federal victory at Mill Springs, Ky.; to the general who saved the day at Stone's River; to the rock of Chickamauga; to the general who crushed the backbone of the rebellion at Nashville, Tenn.; to the general who never lost a battle; and to the man who, in the opinion of his friends, never made a mistake."

Every foot of the battle ground of Nashville was closely contested. Thousands of the Confederate soldiers were Tennesseans. They were in sight of the capital of their native State, within sight of their own firesides, their homes, and their dear ones, but their condition and the superior numbers of the opposing forces in time compelled them to give up the struggle, but not until all hope was gone. The heavy rains in the early part of the month had swollen the streams beyond their banks. This was the condition of Duck River [in Columbia, Tenn.], that must be crossed in the retreat [southward]. Gen. Thomas ordered one of his staff officers back to Nashville to bring the pontoon train out to enable a portion of his army to cross Duck River in advance of Hood, and thereby cut off the retreat of the army that was left and cause it to surrender, but by some unlooked-for error on the part of the officer intrusted with this important mission, he guided the pontoon train out the Murfreesboro Pike until he nearly reached Murfreesboro [50 miles northeast of Columbia] before he discovered his mistake. This great delay gave time for the Confederate forces to make the crossing and continue their march southward.

Duck River sign, Columbia, Tenn. (Photo Lochlainn Seabrook)

It has always been believed, by those familiar with the facts, that, had

Gen. Thomas's orders been successfully and promptly carried out, Gen. Hood's army would have been compelled to surrender, which doubtless would have brought the war to a still earlier ending. The mistake made by Gen. Thomas's staff officer was never officially reported, nor was it indeed known to but a few of the members of the staff.

Gen. Thomas was certainly one of the greatest generals of the Union army. He was a Virginian by birth, a graduate of West Point, a classmate of Gen. Robert E. Lee. It was doubtless a great struggle when the war broke out for Gen. Thomas to decide his future course. Gen. Lee thought his first allegiance was to his native State [Virginia], while Gen. Thomas thought differently, believed he owed his allegiance first to his country, and remained loyal to the Union and became one of its greatest generals, if not the greatest of all the generals in the Union army.

He was known for his exceeding kind-heartedness and his great care for his soldiers. He took a personal interest in their comfort and welfare, and was beloved by all of them. In time of battle his constant thought was to save the lives of all he could, and to make no useless sacrifices. He surrounded himself generally with young men, particularly his personal staff, all of whom, with the exception of one or two, were between the ages of twenty-five and thirty-five. He was like a father to them. Frequently he would call them together and advise with them, cautioning them against excesses of all kinds, and advising them to be merciful to the prisoners of war and to treat them as they would wish to be treated under like circumstances.

A staff officer relates an incident that occurred at headquarters when the General heard that some of the younger members of his staff had been indulging in a game of "draw poker." He summoned them in his presence and told them that he was aware of the attractions of the game among officers of the army, and he said: "I don't mean that you shall not play the game; but if you will, don't play with my provost marshal general" (the latter played a scientific or congressional game that was destructive to the younger set). This officer, Gen. Johnson, had a brother in the Confederate army.

When the war closed there were none more anxious for peace than Gen. Thomas, and he at once set about restoring all the property, buildings, houses, etc., in use by the government to the owners. At that time his headquarters were in Nashville, and he was in command of the military division of the Mississippi. He at once issued peremptory orders to restore to the owners all the buildings occupied by the army. He caused the officers to occupy smaller quarters, to double up, where necessary, in order to surrender to the owners their property, that they might receive the revenue therefrom. He directed and caused to be restored to the corporations all the railroads and railroad properties in his division, and his whole mind seemed to be bent upon restoring peace to the country and to making happy and contented the returned soldiers of the Confederacy. Peace and prosperity and the building up of the country were his watchwords.

Gen. Thomas's innate modesty was one of his great virtues. He believed not in display and honoring the victorious. His sympathy for those who had sacrificed their all was ever manifest. He loved his country and her whole people.

An evidence of Gen. Thomas's modesty and dislike of being lionized occurred soon after the war. Upon his visit to Washington, where he was called on official business, news of his coming had preceded him, much to his discomfort. The morning after his arrival he was called upon by the Mayor of New York and a committee of fifty prominent citizens. He was standing in the vestibule of Willard's Hotel when the committee marched in. The New York Mayor advanced and said that they came from New York to extend an invitation for him to visit their city, that they might lionize him. The General replied: "I thank you kindly for the invitation, but please say to the good people of New York City that when they can receive me as a lamb, and not as a lion, I shall be happy to visit them." The Mayor and his committee were so surprised at the reply that the matter ended there.

One of Gen. Thomas's great hobbies was national cemeteries. He often expressed a desire to see established a national cemetery on every prominent battlefield. He selected the cemetery site near Chattanooga at the time the great battle was being fought, and in obedience to his wishes it was

George H. Thomas, U.S.A.

established on that identical spot after the war. He also selected the location for the National Cemetery near Nashville, Tenn., the land, some sixty-five acres, being intersected by the Louisville and Nashville Railroad, with graves on each side of the track. His desire was, when practicable, to locate all the national cemeteries on lines of railroads or prominent river; that people should ever be reminded of the terrors and fatalities of war.

One exception was made to this rule in Georgia. He desired particularly to locate a cemetery on the Western and Atlantic Road, near Atlanta, but in the several locations presented to the General to select from, there was a beautiful eminence in Marietta, about a half mile back from the

railroad. The place belonged to a Mr. Boyd, a resident of Georgia and a staunch Union man, who insisted upon Gen. Thomas accepting his place as a gift to the government for a national cemetery. The only consideration asked was that the body of the donor should be interred within the cemetery inclosure. The donation was so magnanimous that the General could not decline. The place was selected, and the remains of Mr. Boyd now rest in the national cemetery.[46] — UNION MAJOR A. W. WILLS (staff quartermaster under General George H. Thomas)

Union stronghold Fort Negley, Nashville, Tenn., looking northeast. Photo taken March 1864, ten months before the Battle of Nashville.

WHEN I WAS AT THE BATTLE OF NASHVILLE

☞ It would indeed be a great pleasure to me to visit Nashville again. Of course the Nashville of to-day is very different from Nashville of nearly forty years ago. I was there during the battle. For about three days before, the whole face of the country was a glare of ice. The gunboat *Carondelet*, on which I was serving as paymaster's clerk, lay about three miles below the city, at the right of our armory. One day I walked along our lines from the boat up to Fort Negley. I assure you I had a slippery trip of it. The afternoon of the last day of the battle we were at the landing in the city. I shall never forget the terrible uproar and commotion of that conflict. Above the tumult there was, at regular intervals, a thunderous roar that was said to be the hundred-pound guns of old Negley. It is useless for me to try to describe the scene. The magic touch of pen has never been developed, nor has the tongue been created, that can fitly describe a battle.

I shall never forget a scene I witnessed the day after the battle. I was at the stockade when the Confederate prisoners were brought in. All about the gateway the mud was about eight inches deep and very thin. A Union soldier brought in a prisoner, turned him over to the proper officer, sank down in that thin mud, and in half a minute was fast asleep. Forty-two years ago last August I was wounded at Richmond, Ky. I have suffered more or less ever since.[47] — UNION SOLDIER WARREN R. KING

FLANKING HOOD AT NASHVILLE

☛ Previous to the battle our regiment, the Seventh Minnesota, in the Third Brigade, First Division, Sixteenth Army Corps, lay along the outer line of works in front of Nashville, our right resting on the railroad running to Johnsonville. On the morning of December 15 we marched out through the fog and formed in column of brigades on the left of the Harding Pike, and about a mile and one-half in advance of our works. Here we deployed into line, and I think that our regiment was on the extreme left of our corps. We then marched in line of battle for some distance, when it was discovered that there was a long interval to our left which was unoccupied. We lay here until some time in the afternoon, out of range of small arms, but subject to the fire of a battery on a high point just to the left of the Hillsboro Pike, which was annoying, the guns being well served by experienced gunners. Late in the afternoon we were ordered to storm the works in our front, being stone walls with a redoubt on the right of the Hillsboro Pike, just opposite the battery mentioned above.

We advanced on the run down a gentle slope and through open woods until out of breath, when we lay down for a few minutes; then we ran down across a little brook and lay down under cover of the slope ascending to the

State Capitol, Nashville, Tenn.; occupied as Fort (Andrew) Johnson by Union forces, 1862-1865.

redoubt. We went into the redoubt, or such portion of our regiment as fronted on it did, which included my company. Of course all of this was not done without opposition on the part of the Confederates. We suffered from the direct fire from the works assaulted, and also from a cross fire, enfilading our line part of the time, from the fort on the hill across the pike.

We had scarcely gained possession of the works when the fort across the way opened upon us, not regarding the fact that there were about as many Confederates with us inside of the redoubt as there were of our own men.

It is almost a miracle that any one was left alive in that redoubt, for the gunners cut their fuses so that every shell burst inside of it, and there did not seem to be ten seconds' interval between the discharges. Col. S. G. Hill, our brigade commander, gave the order to charge the fort on the hill, and was shot through the head the next moment. Our major heard the order and repeated it; we jumped down from the wall, and, led by Col. Marshall, crossed the pike and climbed the hill, the Confederates leaving the fort as we got to it. We followed on through the woods until dusk, when we bivouacked for the night. As we followed the Confederates who evacuated the fort on the hill, we did not leave any one to take possession of the guns, and I saw a line of our troops advancing toward it from the front, but several hundred yards distant. They bravely marched up to it and

"A brisk cannonading was being carried on over our heads."

carried the works, and received the credit, which their commander claimed in his report, and which, so far as I know, was never disputed, as the reports were never seen until published by the government.

I have just looked over the reports of Col. Wolfe, commanding the Third Brigade, Second Division, Detachment [Union] Army of the Tennessee (by which we were designated at Nashville instead of Sixteenth Corps), and find he claims that his skirmishers captured the fort; but from Gen. Smith's report it seems that the Fourth Corps captured it. It might be interesting to ascertain how many guns were captured at Nashville, taking the statements of our generals and subordinate commanders as being correct.

Although tired out with the day's experiences, the night was so cold that I could get no continuous sleep. We were aroused long before daylight of the 16th and made a long and weary march, hailing at some newly constructed works, probably the abandoned Confederate line of the day before. Here we halted, but in a few moments an orderly rode up on the gallop, and the next moment the bugle sounded the "assembly," followed by the "march."

. . . We swung to the right, with my company on the "moving flank," and it was hard work to get through the woods; but finally we came out to a road, crossing which we went into a field and into a ravine which led up to the rear of the "Bradford House." In this ravine we stopped to catch our breath, and found it a good place to be in, as a brisk cannonading was being carried on over our heads, one of my men being wounded from a piece of shell while resting there.

Directly the regiment began moving to the right by the flank, and as my position in line of battle when on the march was on the left of my company, and as the ravine was narrow and the company strung out in single file, it took me some time to run to the head, which saved my life, for when within about twenty feet of my proper position, the regiment coming out of the ravine on to the grounds around the "Bradford House," a shell from the [Confederate] Pointe Coupee Battery (Louisiana Troops) burst and killed the rear man of the company in front of mine and the first man of my company.

We went into line at right angles to the Granny White Pike, our left slightly in advance of the house, but a little to the right of it, the Twelfth Iowa being between us and the pike. Here we lay in the rain skirmishing until about 3 P.M., when we saw one of our regiments on the extreme right of our line (on Shy's Hill) begin a charge on the Confederate works. As we saw them go over the works and heard the cheering we realized that the business was "catching," and that in a few minutes we would have to do the same thing.

Lawn of the Overton Lea House, from where Hood directed his troops.

About the time the first regiment had reached the Confederate works the next one to it started, and in that order they kept on until but a short distance away from us, when our colonel, who was commanding the brigade that day, rode from our right and rear and ordered us to charge.

We rose and, throwing down the fence, advanced on the run until we reached the Confederate rifle pits, made of rails, where we halted for breath. The field was a hard one to travel over, the mud being ankle deep. Directly we advanced, the regiment obliqued to the right to get through the only gap in the wall; in fact, the only one for a long distance either way. My company was directly in front of the Pointe Coupee Battery, which had poured grape, canister, and shrapnel into us from the moment we started, and the supporting line had also done their share with their rifles. The works, a stone wall built up very high, with rails laid a part of the way from the top and sloping to the ground toward us, had no opening in our front, except a slight notch at the top, just to the left of the battery.

The greater portion of my company had, as was right, "touched elbows"

Photo from in front of the Nashville Capitol Building, dated December 15, 1864.

to the right, while ten or twelve had touched to the left; and, as I was looking to the front, calculating how we could get over the wall, I had not noticed the oblique movement. As soon as I saw it, there being a wide gap in my company, I told the boys that we would go right ahead. We reached the wall just as the "break" came, and the notch in the wall was so high, and I was so badly used up with a stitch in the side, that the boys had to boost me up to the notch, through which I climbed and dropped to the ground just as my colonel came along inside the line on the gallop, calling out [to the Confederate soldiers]: "Lay down your arms and surrender." There were but four or five men in the battery, one the commander, Capt. Alcide Bouanchaud, and they had ceased resisting. I told the men who were with me to follow me, and went to the support of my colonel, who was entirely alone and surrounded by, apparently, thousands of the Confederates.

In the morning, before we advanced, I had told my second lieutenant, James B. Turrittin, that, in the event of our capturing any cannon that day, to take a guard and stay with them. This he did, as our company, after getting inside of the works, advancing by the left flank, were the first to reach the battery. And now I learn from "history," if the reports of officers are history, that the brigade directly on our right captured the battery; and, in fact, the brigade commander, with his staff, rode down and ordered my lieutenant to take his men and rejoin his regiment. But the lieutenant told him flatly that he would only be relieved by his own officers. . . . The two brigade commanders got together—I think they were politicians—and agreed to divide the guns, each taking two.

I also learn from the same source that the command on my left, which did not start until after we did, also captured those same guns; and they even went one better, for one of their men captured (?) the guidon [pennant] of the battery, and received notice in general orders and a Congressional medal for bravery in action—all of which should teach soldiers that, when they capture anything, they should rummage around and see that there is not anything left lying on the ground, and take the whole aggregation with them. Such is glory.

Now, I never thought much about the glory business until since I began to read history from the "Rebellion Records." I now see how it is done.

I forgot to say in the proper place that there was no intention of charging the Confederates on the 16th, as we had received orders to intrench, and our details sent for intrenching tools had nearly reached our lines when the charge took place. Besides, Col. Marshall told me a few days after, that he went to Gen. Smith's headquarters and urged the General to make a charge, that the General said: "No, there will be no charge. We are going to intrench." While talking he heard the noise of the charge, the increased fire, and the cheering, and he said to the General, "They are charging now," to which the General replied: "No, I don't understand that there is to be a charge." But the Colonel did not wait for any more words—he put spurs to his horse and dashed up, as I have described, and ordered the charge.[48] — UNION CAPTAIN THEODORE G. CARTER (7th Minnesota Infantry)

THE UNION ARMY & HOOD'S RETREAT

☛ Night was falling when the victory was complete, and a drenching rain had set in to add to the darkness and confusion. Thomas ordered Wood to pursue by the Franklin road, and the cavalry by the Granny White road, to the intersection with that to Franklin, when Wilson was to take the advance. Smith and Schofield were ordered to follow Wilson on the next day. But few, if any, of the Confederates fled by the Granny White turnpike, for it was commanded by Wilson's cavalry, and the masses streamed through the Brentwood Hills, making the best of their way to the Franklin road.

Harpeth River sign, Franklin, Tenn. (Photo Lochlainn Seabrook)

There was hardly the semblance of organization among them till they passed the Harpeth River. Forrest was ordered to retreat on Shelbyville and Pulaski, but he hurried Armstrong's brigade of cavalry across country to get in rear of Hood's routed forces and cover their retreat. Reynolds's and Coleman's brigades had been taken from the line, at the last moment, to cover the passes through the Brentwood Hills from the Granny White road, and had preserved their organization. By delaying the advance of Wilson's horsemen toward the Franklin turnpike, these brigades had saved the larger part of Hood's army from capture.

The hospitals at Franklin were abandoned, containing over two thousand wounded. Wilson, with his cavalry, had come up with the rear guard four miles north of Franklin, at Hollow Tree Gap, and Knipe's division, charging it in front and flank, carried the position, capturing over four hundred prisoners and their colors. At the Harpeth, Johnson's division crossed some distance below, and compelled Hood to abandon the defence of the river at Franklin. At Rutherford Creek, on the 18th, the water was up, the stream was a torrent, and some delay in getting a pontoon train forward gave the enemy a little respite.

At Columbia [on December 18], Forrest rejoined Hood, and his cavalry, with an infantry rear guard under command of Walthall, covered the retreat to the Tennessee. General Walthall's force was made up of the two brigades which had been detached with Forrest, and of three others besides his own division. This force was able to present so strong a front that, aided by the condition of the roads and streams, which retarded pursuit, our advance guard was not able to break through again, and Hood reached the Tennessee [River], at Bainbridge, by way of Pulaski, on the 26th. Here he was favored by a gleam of good fortune in the arrival of

Rutherford Creek, Spring Hill, Tenn. This small bucolic river played a central role in the battles leading up to Nashville and Hood's subsequent retreat. (Photo Lochlainn Seabrook)

pontoons, which had been floated down from Decatur, where, by some blunder, they had been left by our forces when General Granger had evacuated that post in November. Their own pontoon train was delayed by the condition of the roads, and part of the defeated army passed the Tennessee before it arrived; but when it came it was laid, and Hood had his shattered forces on the southern bank by the evening of the 27th.

A Confederate account states that soon after the first bridge was down, two National [Union] gunboats appeared in the direction of Florence and steamed toward it; but General [Alexander P.] Stewart opened upon them with a battery of smooth field guns, which was all he then had, and the boats desisted from the attempt to break through the pontoons.

From Franklin, on the 17th, Thomas had ordered Steedman to march to Murfreesboro, and thence to proceed by rail to Decatur, occupying the posts in Northern Alabama which had been abandoned earlier in the campaign. At the close of the month Steedman was at Decatur, Wood was near Lexington, in North Alabama, thirty miles southwest of Pulaski, Smith was at Pulaski, and Schofield at Columbia. Thomas issued his orders announcing the close of the campaign, assigning winter quarters to the various corps; but directions were received from Washington to continue operations. The expected march of Sherman northward, from Savannah, made it important that no rest or time for concentration should be given the enemy in the Gulf States, and Thomas prepared for a new campaign.

Among the results of the two days' battle at Nashville had been the capture of about four thousand five hundred prisoners, and fifty-three pieces of artillery, besides small arms in great number. Among the [Confederate] prisoners were Generals Johnson, Smith, Jackson, and Rucker, and a number of regimental officers commanding brigades. The losses in killed and wounded on both sides were small, compared with the material results, though the demoralization of Hood's army, followed so soon by the close of the war, leaves us without the full returns which are necessary to determine the casualties on the Confederate side.

Hood witnessed the first break in his lines at this spot.

Hood assembled the remnant of his army at Tupelo, Mississippi, and then gave furloughs to part of his men (particularly the Tennesseans), and asked to be relieved from the command of the army. He does not admit a loss from all causes, from December 15th to 30th, as great as the number of prisoners taken by Thomas's army on the 15th and 16th, and claims that he reassembled at Tupelo an army of 18,500 effective muskets. These figures are nearly worthless for any historical purpose. General Thomas's return of prisoners captured, and deserters received during November and December, show the number to be over thirteen thousand; besides these he reports the capture of 72, cannon and 3,000 muskets. We shall meet with some of the veterans of Hood's army again in the Carolinas, maintaining their old corps organization; but, for the time, they were scattered and demoralized, and seemed almost to lose the character of a disciplined army.

Thomas's losses in the battle of Nashville were 3,057, of which less than four hundred were killed. The analysis of these figures shows that the Fourth Corps suffered a little less than a thousand casualties, of which two-thirds were in the unsuccessful attack upon Overton's Hill. Steedman's losses were over eight hundred, and nearly all of them seem to have occurred in the same assault, those of his second colored brigade (Colonel Thompson's) being fifty per cent heavier than in any other on the field. The Sixteenth Corps lost 750, which appear to have been pretty evenly divided between the two days. It is noteworthy that the attack upon the angle at Shy's Hill was not a costly one, for the preceding preparation by the enfilading artillery fire, and the shape of the ground, which enabled McMillan to approach closely before exposing his men, show that success in such cases (when success is possible), follows the use of proper means. The total number of casualties in McMillan's brigade was 118, of which not more than two-thirds occurred in the final assault, and they were less than half of those which occurred in Hubbard's brigade, which went forward on its left against the works in the lower ground, and where Bate's centre and right, holding on with better cover, were able to inflict considerable loss before the crushing of the whole of Hood's left made their position untenable.

The Twenty-third Corps was in reserve nearly all of the first day, and its only losses worth mentioning were in Couch's division, when carrying the hill close to Shy's in the evening. The position was of inestimable importance for one so cheaply gained, for the casualties were only 150. Those of the other division in the final assault were less than twenty. As nearly always happens in a panic, the break of the enemy's line was so sudden and complete that the loss was almost wholly on one side. The loss in the cavalry corps was 329, and when distributed among the three divisions, it must also be regarded as trifling, and the larger part, even of this, undoubtedly occurred in carrying the redoubts on the 15th.

These considerations show that the success was due chiefly to the tactical combination of a superior force, and that moral causes, growing out of the preceding part of the campaign, must have had a great effect in producing discouragement among Hood's men, and predisposing them to panic when the break in the line occurred. Hood was evidently in fault, as a tactician, on the 15th, when he allowed Thomas to array his whole force diagonally beyond his left flank, and awaited an attack in such a position. His only hope was to have drawn back to the Brentwood Hills at once, without allowing his troops to become engaged. He would thus have saved them from the demoralizing effect of being driven from position after position on the first day, and from the conviction (which was partly the cause of its own fulfilment) that they were wholly unable to cope with the National [Union] army. On the morning of the 16th he issued orders to his subordinates to prepare for a retreat in the evening; but he could not withdraw under fire, and the decision was reached too late to be of successful accomplishment. The evening found his routed army a disorganized crowd flying from the lost battle-field.

Hood's retreat from Nashville to the Tennessee [River] and Thomas's pursuit were almost equally laborious for their armies, though very different in their effect upon the spirits of the troops. The roads were in horrible condition, even those which had been macadamized being almost impassable. The ordinary country roads were much worse, and, after passing Pulaski, till the Tennessee was reached, the wrecks of wagons and the carcasses of animals filled the way. Hood had been forced to destroy ammunition to get teams to take forward his pontoons, and Wilson and Wood in pursuit had been obliged to leave most of their cannon, and double the teams of the rest. On getting orders from Washington to resume the campaign, Thomas ordered Wood to assemble the Fourth Corps at Huntsville, Ala., Schofield, Smith, and Wilson to concentrate at Eastport, Mississippi. Schofield marched the Twenty-third Corps to Clifton on the Tennessee, preparatory to taking boats up the river, but other orders met him there, transferring him to a distant field upon the sea-coast.

Shy's Hill, where the Confederate line was shattered.

The completeness of the victory at Nashville caused a joyful revulsion of feeling throughout the Northern States. The impatience of the President and of General Grant had only been the expression of a feeling which all the country had shared. The conviction was general that Hood ought to have been met much nearer the Tennessee River, and the fear that he would be allowed to march to the Ohio was all but universal. Now, however, all vied in giving honor to the successful general, and not a few were ready to blame the authorities at Washington for having doubted, even for a day, the wisdom of Thomas's management of the early campaign.

The President, the Secretary of War, and General Grant were not slow or stinting in their congratulations, and between the chief actors in the scene a cordial good understanding was at once established. On the one hand, it was ungrudgingly conceded that the final battle had been skillfully delivered and crowned with the most satisfactory results; on the other, it was felt that the anxiety of the early December days was reasonable, and that the demand for prompt action was such a stimulus to great exertion as the responsible authorities of a government may apply to its most trusted officers in such a crisis, without giving cause for lasting chagrin. In such a time, the reward for success and the responsibility for ill-fortune may neither of them be quite justly proportioned to real desert, and both are apt to be exaggerated. In war, more than in anything else, the proverb "all's well that ends well" is the popular one, and the popular sympathy was evidently with the hero of the great victory.

Few men have the qualities which deserve public confidence in greater measure than General Thomas. He was a patriot whose love of his country was greater than his attachment to a province;[49] a Virginian who refused to follow the example of [Robert E.] Lee in taking arms against the National Government which Washington had founded.[50] He [Thomas] was a man of large mould in body and mind, of a quiet, modest dignity, who hated pretence, and avoided notoriety. He was transparently true to his superiors, and kindly considerate to his subordinates. He had the personal courage which would be ashamed of its own display as much as of a cowardice, but which seemed simply oblivious of danger when duty required a risk to be taken. These qualities made him always a trusted lieutenant to his chief, and were the basis of an affectionate and respectful attachment in his own army which was peculiar.

Rains Place, Nashville, Tenn. According to Confederate soldiers, during the battle hundreds of black Yankees were killed and injured here, yet their white Union officers were nowhere to be seen.

His real and unaffected aversion to taking the chief responsibility of command had kept him in secondary positions when his rank in both the regular and volunteer armies would have made him the head of a separate army in the field. In this respect he was not unlike [William J.] Hardee, in the Confederate Army, who also steadily refused a supreme command. The duties of the soldier, and the exhibition of courage and skill in making the details of a campaign successful, were easy to him; but to become the theme of discussion in Congress and in the newspapers, to be the butt of ten thousand public critics, and to carry the burden of plans whose failure might be ruin to the country—this he hated so heartily and shrunk from so naturally, that, after all his long experience, we have seen him protesting that the position assigned him in this last campaign was "the one thing he did not want." That these qualities in some degree unfitted him for an independent command cannot be questioned. The very anxiety to be right, if it is excessive, produces hesitation in action and timidity in plan. Under such conditions the stimulus from without, coming in the form of urgency from the Government and command from the General-in-Chief, may not have been wholly unwelcome, and unquestionably added vigor to the final movements.

It is, however, in the earlier part of the campaign that the steps taken were most open to question, though very few of the officers and men who served there had any exact knowledge of the means which were at General Thomas's disposal, or of the manner in which they were used. The magnitude of the final success was so splendid, that it seemed to prove each step toward it the best possible; and it is only when we examine the official evidence of the number and position of the troops in Tennessee that we are able to apply to the events which followed the tests afforded by the rules of military art.

General Thomas tells us in his official report that, had Hood delayed his advance from Florence ten days longer, he would have met him at Columbia, or some other point south of the Duck River. An early concentration in front of the enemy is thus indicated as the controlling purpose, and Hood's march on Nashville is recognized as the result only of the unforeseen delays in the arrival of General Smith with his divisions. The military student of the campaign is therefore led to inquire whether a concentration of the means at hand would not have opposed to Hood a force which would have kept him at least south of Duck River till Smith could have arrived.

Communication with Sherman was broken on November 12th, and Hood began his advance from Florence on the 20th, though it was not till the 26th that his infantry was all assembled in front of Columbia, Schofield having abandoned Pulaski on the 22nd. A fortnight was thus unexpectedly given for concentration, and the

Southern patriot Col. John Overton, owner of Travellers' Rest, Nashville, Tenn.

resources of the railways were at Thomas's disposal. His tri-monthly return of November 20th shows a force in Tennessee of 59,534 officers and men "present for duty equipped." To determine the deductions necessary for smaller garrisons and bridge guards, no better method can be used than to make them the same as was actually done when the battle of Nashville was imminent. Add to these a garrison of 2,500 for Nashville and Chattanooga each, and we shall find still remaining a force of 47,000 infantry and artillery, and about six thousand cavalry, which there could have been no difficulty in assembling at Columbia before Hood reached there.

After Sherman started from Rome, it was known that Wheeler's cavalry had hastened after him. The raid of Breckenridge into East Tennessee was a feeble diversion which the troops in that part of Schofield's department were quite able to meet. Roddey's division of cavalry was the only Confederate force in North Alabama, and gave no trouble during the campaign. Everything combined, therefore, to point to an immediate concentration in front of Hood as the true policy on our side. General R. S. Granger was at Decatur on November 1st with over five thousand men. Steedman could have joined him there with the five thousand which he subsequently took to Nashville. The bridge and trestle between Pulaski and Athens could have been rebuilt, and if demonstrations on the south of the Tennessee did not keep Hood from committing himself to a campaign north of the river, the divisions of Steedman and Granger could have joined Schofield at Pulaski. If Thomas had joined them there or at Columbia with the remainder of his available force, he would have been superior to Hood in everything but cavalry from the beginning, and would have been able himself to dictate whether a battle should be fought before the arrival of Smith's corps.

From the knowledge of the facts we now have, it would seem that Thomas gave undue importance to the necessity of having the Sixteenth Corps present before decisive operations against Hood. When the battle of Nashville was fought, Rousseau's eight thousand or more at Murfreesboro were as wholly out of the account as if they had been north of the Ohio, and nearly five thousand of Cruft's division, besides the post garrison, were kept in the works at the city with General Donaldson's employees, and were not brought into the action. The battle was fought, therefore, with a force numerically less than it would have been if Smith's corps had been entirely absent, and Rousseau and Cruft had been in line instead.

It is true that a good many new regiments had taken the place of old ones; but these were not what is commonly meant by raw recruits. They were always officered by men of experience, and many veterans were in the ranks. Four thousand of them swelled the old divisions of the Fourth Corps, and there was no complaint that they did not fight well. As to the provisional organization of convalescents and furloughed men of the

Samuel E. Opdycke, U.S.A.

different corps with Sherman, their conduct in Grosvenor's brigade in this action, and subsequently on the North Carolina coast, proved they were scarcely distinguishable from veteran troops under their accustomed flags. But if the troops had not been of the best quality, there would be no less need of handling them according to the principles which military experience has established, and a rapid concentration would still be proper.

Travellers' Rest, Hood's headquarters during part of the Battle of Nashville. (Photo Lochlainn Seabrook)

When Hood began the campaign in earnest, the first movements of our forces were the reverse of concentric. Granger, instead of joining Schofield, was sent a hundred miles to the east, and the garrison at Johnsonville was taken to the rear of Nashville. This would seem to have been with the idea that it was necessary to protect the railways against expected raids. If so, it was an error, for *had Hood been unwise enough to have detached Forrest for such a purpose, he would have been at the same disadvantage he subsequently was at Nashville, where the absence of the hostile cavalry made the opportunity which resulted so gloriously for our arms.* No raid of Forrest's could have done more damage to the Chattanooga Railroad than the forced retreat from Pulaski did to an equally important line, to say nothing of the damage actually done to the former while Hood lay in front of Nashville.

The delay in concentration was also fraught with the very gravest perils to the portion of the army under Schofield. It was Hood's policy to force the fighting with this, in the hope of destroying or capturing it before it could be aided, yet nothing was farther from Thomas's wish than that it should make a precipitate retreat. Had it reached Nashville a single day sooner, Thomas would have been wholly unprepared to meet his adversary, and Steedman's reinforcements would have been cut off. To save time, Schofield took the gravest risks; but as he well said, the slightest mistake on his part, or the failure of a subordinate, might have proved disastrous. The misconduct of Wagner at Franklin would certainly have proved so, but for the heroism of Opdycke and White and the brave men of their commands.

A consideration of all the facts, therefore, seems to show that Thomas should have concentrated every available man in front of Hood before the latter moved; and that the great success of the closing part of the campaign was in spite of this error in its beginning, and by no means because of it. The difficulties had certainly been very great, and to an ordinary man they would have been overwhelming. There was a great scarcity of animals for the cavalry, for the artillery, for the pontoons, and for the wagon trains, while the season was such as to use up the animals with double rapidity. The army was new to its organization, and though it did all that an army could do, Thomas could hardly have full faith in it till it had been proven. But through all these difficulties a triumph was achieved which has been rarely equalled, and without which even Sherman's position in the heart of the Confederacy and on the communications of its only remaining great army must have lost half its significance.[51] — UNION GENERAL JACOB DOLSON COX

GEN. THOMAS' OFFICIAL REPORT AFTER NASHVILLE

☛ Headquarters Department of the Cumberland, Six Miles from Nashville, December 16, 1864. To the President of the United States, Hon. E. M. Stanton, and General U. S. Grant, Washington:

This army thanks you for your approbation of its conduct yesterday, and, to assure you that it is not misplaced, I have the honor to report that the enemy has been pressed at all points to-day on his line of retreat through the Brentwood Hills, and Brigadier-General Hatch, of Wilson's Corps of Cavalry, on the right, turned the enemy's left and captured a large number of prisoners; number not yet reported. Major General Schofield's troops, next on the left of cavalry, carried several heights, captured many prisoners and six pieces of artillery. Brevet Major-General Smith, next on the left of Major-General Schofield, carried the salient point of the enemy's line with McWilliams's brigade of McArthur's division, capturing 16 pieces of artillery, 2 brigadier-generals, and about 2000 prisoners.

Brigadier-General Garrard's division of Smith's command, next on the left of McArthur's division, carried the enemy's intrenchments, capturing all the artillery and troops on the line. Brigadier-General Wood's, on the Franklin pike, took up the assault, carried the enemy's intrenchments in

Ulysses S. Grant, U.S.A.

his front, captured 8 pieces, something over 600 prisoners, and drove the enemy to within one mile of Brentwood Pass. Major-General Steedman, commanding detachments of the Military Division of the Mississippi, most nobly supported General Wood's left, and bore a most honorable part in the operations of the day.

I have ordered the pursuit [of Hood] to be continued in the morning at daylight, although the troops are very much fatigued. The greatest enthusiasm prevails.

I must not forget to report the operations of Brigadier-General R. W. Johnson in successfully driving the enemy, with co-operation of the gunboats under Lieutenant-Commander Fitch, from their established batteries on the

Cumberland River below the city of Nashville, and the services of Brigadier-General Croxton's brigade in covering and relieving our right and rear in the operations of yesterday and to-day. Although I have no report of the number of prisoners captured by Johnson's and Croxton's commands, I know they have made a large number. I am glad to be able to state that the number of prisoners captured yesterday greatly exceeds the number reported by me last evening. The roads, fields, and intrenchments are strewn with the enemy's abandoned small-arms, abandoned in their retreat.

In conclusion, I am happy to state that all this has been effected with but a very small loss to us. Our loss does not probably exceed three thousand, very few killed.[52] — UNION GENERAL GEORGE HENRY THOMAS (commander, U.S. forces)

Union forces, outer lines, Nashville, Tenn., December 16, 1864.

APPENDIX

FROM AN ADDRESS BY THE NASHVILLE
NATIONAL BATTLEFIELD ASSOCIATION

1909

The Nashville National Battlefield Association is organized for the purpose of locating and permanently marking the positions of the different organizations of the armies of both sides during the progress of the battle which took place near Nashville on December 15 and 16, 1864. The plow and the harrow have obliterated much of the earthworks which once stretched across the fields, woods, and hills just south of the city. At some points where the land is broken the intrenchments are still quite distinct; but in open fields, yards, and gardens they are rarely noticed.

Our purpose is to cause the positions on the days of the battle to be so mapped as to show not only roads, etc., as they then existed, but also show the present roads and objects, old landmarks to be distinguished, however, by distinctive marking. It is desired to have the notable positions marked by granite or bronze markers.

The Association will ask the United States to put up these markers and also to construct driveways or roads connecting the public highways, so that views of the battlefield can be better obtained. The government will also be asked to make a national park out of at least a part of this battlefield.

All persons of legal age may be members of the Association, whether residents of Tennessee or not, upon payment of $5 for one year's membership to Mr. A. H. Robinson, Treasurer, American National Bank. Any one will be qualified to be balloted on as a member. It is desired that those who are interested in this object will so apply for membership. Ladies will be received into membership.

The battle of Nashville was the decisive battle of the war, as it practically destroyed the army [of Tennessee, C.S.A.] which for four years had defended the west and rear of Lee. This is in no sense to celebrate the defeat. Many feats of heroism were exhibited in this last important struggle. It is the history of the battle at our doors that we wish to preserve.

The land upon which the battle of Nashville was fought is far too valuable for an extended park; but it is desired that a national park shall be made out of some central or otherwise important part of the field, that driveways be opened and built so as to properly connect the system of roads, and that all chief points be durably marked. It is expected that different State organizations may erect handsome commemorative monuments.

The $5 annual dues will be used for the expenses that are necessarily incident to the undertaking.

It is hoped that a large number of men and women will send the dues to the Treasurer and apply for membership. They will not be asked for any money besides the membership fee of $5.

The officers of the Association are: President, Ex-Gov. James D. Porter; Vice Presidents, Gen. G. P. Thruston and Maj. W. F. Foster; Secretary, M. B. Morton; Treasurer, A. H. Robinson; Executive Committee: Maj. A. W. Wills, Capt. John W. Morton, G. H. Baskette, S. A. Cunningham, Leland Hume, R. L. Burch, and Capt. J. L. Hill.[53]

NOTES

1. Woods, p. 47.

2. On Lincoln's socialistic, Marxist, and communist thoughts, ideas, and tendencies, see my books: 1) *Lincoln's War: The Real Cause, The Real Winner, the Real Loser*; 2) *Abraham Lincoln Was a Liberal, Jefferson Davis Was a Conservative: The Missing Key to Understanding the American Civil War*; 3) *Abraham Lincoln: The Southern View*. Also see McCarty, passim; Browder, passim; Benson and Kennedy, passim.

3. See J. W. Jones, TDMV, pp. 144, 200-201, 273.

4. See Seabrook, TAHSR, passim. See also, Pollard, LC, p. 178; J. H. Franklin, pp. 101, 111, 130, 149; Nicolay and Hay, ALCW, Vol. 1, p. 627.

5. BISG (the "Book Industry Study Group"), for example—a Left-wing organization which describes itself as "the leading book trade association for standardized best practices, research and information, and events"—gives its BISAC ("Book Industry Standards and Communications") listing for works on the War for Southern Independence under the heading "Civil War Period, 1850-1877." Nearly all books published in the U.S.A. today are under the categorizational control of this progressive group located in New York City.

6. See e.g., Seabrook, TQJD, pp. 30, 38, 76.

7. See e.g., J. Davis, RFCG, Vol. 1, pp. 55, 422; Vol. 2, pp. 4, 161, 454, 610. Besides using the term "Civil War" himself, President Davis cites numerous other individuals who use it as well.

8. See e.g., *Confederate Veteran*, March 1912, p. 122.

9. Minutes of the Eighth Annual Meeting, July 1898, p. 87.

10. For more on the nihilistic, atheistic, anti-life, anti-tradition, anti-American, anti-Constitution, anti-capitalism, anti-South agenda of the Victorian Republican Party (then the Liberal Party) and the modern Democrat Party (now the Liberal Party), otherwise known as "The Communist/Socialist Rules forteran Revolution," see Hasselberg, pp. 2350-2351; Lenin, passim; Marx and Engels, passim; B. Dodd, passim.

11. *Confederate Veteran*, July 1901, p. 318.

12. For more on this topic, see my book: *Abraham Lincoln Was a Liberal, Jefferson Davis Was a Conservative: The Missing Key to Understanding the American Civil War*.

13. Evans, Vol. 8, pp. 144-145.

14. For more on these battles, see Seabrook, TBOSH; Seabrook, EOTBOF; Seabrook, TMOCP.

15. For more on this topic, see Seabrook, AWAITBLA; Seabrook, LW; Seabrook, ALWALJDWAC.

16. For a full discussion of the Battle of Spring Hill, see Seabrook, TBOSH.

17. Hood, pp. 299-311.

18. *Confederate Veteran*, January 1905, pp. 28-30.

19. *Confederate Veteran*, January 1905, p. 30.

20. It is interesting to note that Steedman, from Pennsylvania, was a rare Yankee Conservative, a pariah in the Liberal North. His traditional politics (which actually made him more Southern than Northern) interfered with and even delayed military promotion, among other issues.

21. We see here the discontentment of Hood's men concerning some of the decisions he made earlier in Georgia, prior to the Tennessee Campaign. Behind this was quite probably their unhappiness with the fact that their former commander Gen. J. E. Johnston had been replaced by Hood.

22. *Confederate Veteran*, January 1909, pp. 17-21. My emphasis.

23. *Confederate Veteran*, April 1909, p. 159.

24. *Confederate Veteran*, April 1904, pp. 269-272. Note: The title of this entry is my own. L.S.

25. *Confederate Veteran*, June 1904, p. 274. Note: The title of this entry is my own. L.S.

26. *Confederate Veteran*, April 1896, p. 106. Note: The title of this entry is my own. L.S.

27. *Confederate Veteran*, July 1903, p. 327. Note: The title of this entry is my own. L.S.

28. *Confederate Veteran*, April 1899, p. 154.

29. *Confederate Veteran*, July 1899, p. 311.

30. *Confederate Veteran*, December 1897, p. 623. Note: The title of this entry is my own. L.S.

31. *Confederate Veteran*, April 1909, Pp. 164-165. My emphasis. Note: The title of this entry is my own. L.S.

32. Evans, Vol. 8, pp. 166-171. My emphasis.

33. *Confederate Veteran*, July 1904, pp. 348-349.

34. Original note by *Confederate Veteran* editor (and founder) Sumner A. Cunningham: "While the worst blunder of the war occurred at Spring Hill, the *Veteran* in copying this extract does not concur in the censure of any officer, unless it be Gen. Hood himself."

35. *Confederate Veteran*, July 1904, pp. 350-353.

36. *Confederate Veteran*, October 1904, pp. 484-485.

37. *Confederate Veteran*, November 1904, pp. 531-532.

38. *Confederate Veteran*, January 1909, pp. 11-13.

39. This is false. According to Hood, when he entered Nashville he had only 20,000 men. *Vida supra*, p. 34.

40. Sending Forrest to Murfreesboro was, in my opinion, Hood's worst decision (of the many he made) during his entire Tennessee Campaign. L.S.

41. Cox, pp. 99-123. Note: The title of this entry is my own. L.S.

42. According to Hood, the Union had 82,000 men at Nashville, the Confederacy only 20,000. As a Southern historian I accept Hood's numbers as the most probable. *Vide supra*, p. 34.

43. So called after the gallant Colonel [William M.] Shy of the 37th Georgia, slain there in the decisive charge which wrecked the Confederate left. (Fiske's original note.)

44. Again we must note that these figures vary considerably from those given by the Confederacy.

45. Fiske, pp. 346-357. Note: The title of this entry is my own, and is based on the views of the writer Fiske. Though not a Union soldier, he described himself as a "Connecticut Yankee" who, while respecting the South and her military men, sympathized entirely with the Union and her primary leaders Grant and Sherman.

46. *Confederate Veteran*, June 1904, pp. 274-276. My emphasis. Note: The title of this entry is my own. L.S.

47. *Confederate Veteran*, June 1904, p. 276. Note: The title of this entry is my own. L.S.

48. *Confederate Veteran*, December 1904, pp. 585-586.

49. Sarcastically referring to the states as "provinces" illustrates the lack of understanding Victorian Yankee Liberals had when it came to the South and to the original Conservative constitutional principles (such as states' rights) that had been carefully constructed and developed by the Founding Generation.

50. Like most other partisan Yankee Liberals then as today, Cox was completely ignorant of authentic history. "The National government which Washington had founded" was a Conservative government, one based on the Conservative principles of a Conservative document: the U.S. Constitution. Republican Lincoln, a Liberal (the parties were reversed in the 1860s) who initiated what would later become the IRS (among numerous other Left-wing departments and programs), and whose administration and army were filled with sycophantic socialists, evinced nothing but disdain for our original government and our original Constitution, and publicly proclaimed his intent to liberalize both. By seceding, the Conservative South demonstrated her resistance to Lincoln's radical goal to alter our government, triggering his anger and his call for the invasion of Dixie. It was thus the Conservative South (then embodied by the Democrat Party), that was fighting for "the government which Washington founded," not the Liberal North. For more on these topics, see Seabrook, LW; Seabrook, ALWALJDWAC.

51. Cox, pp. 124-136. My emphasis. Note: The title of this entry is my own. L.S.

52. R. W. Johnson, pp. 198-200.

53. *Confederate Veteran*, February 1909, p. 53.

BIBLIOGRAPHY

And Suggested Reading

Ashe, Captain Samuel A'Court. *A Southern View of the Invasion of the Southern States and War of 1861-1865*. 1935. Crawfordville, GA: Ruffin Flag Co., 1938 ed.

Benson, Al, Jr., and Walter Donald Kennedy. *Lincoln's Marxists*. Gretna, LA: Pelican, 2011.

Boyd, James P. *Parties, Problems, and Leaders of 1896: An Impartial Presentation of Living National Questions*. Chicago, IL: Publishers' Union, 1896.

Brock, Robert Alonzo (ed.). *Southern Historical Society Papers*. 52 vols. Richmond, VA: Southern Historical Society, 1876-1943.

Browder, Earl. *Lincoln and the Communists*. New York, NY: Workers Library Publishers, Inc., 1936.

Bryan, William Jennings. *The First Battle: A Story of the Campaign of 1896*. Chicago, IL: W. B. Conkey Co., 1896.

Burgess, John William. *The Civil War and the Constitution, 1859-1865*. 2 vols. New York, NY: Charles Scribner's Sons, 1910.

Burns, James MacGregor. *The Vineyard of Liberty*. New York, NY: Alfred A. Knopf, 1982.

Campaigns in Kentucky and Tennessee, Including the Battle of Chickamauga, 1862-1864. Papers of the Military Historical Society of Massachusetts, Vol. 7. Boston, MA: The Military Historical Society of Massachusetts, 1908.

Christian, George Llewellyn. *Abraham Lincoln: An Address Delivered Before R. E. Lee Camp, No. 1 Confederate Veterans at Richmond, VA, October 29, 1909*. Richmond, VA: L. H. Jenkins, 1909.

——. *A Capitol Disaster: A Chapter of Reconstruction in Virginia*. Richmond, VA: self-published, 1915.

——. *Confederate Memories and Experiences*. Richmond, VA: self-published, 1915.

Clare, Israel Smith. *Illustrated History of All Nations*. 15 vols. New York, NY: The Christian Herald, 1909.

Collins, R. M. *Chapters From the Unwritten History of the War Between the States; or, The Incidents in the Life of a Confederate Soldier in Camp, on the March, in the Great Battles, and in Prison*. St. Louis, MO: self-published, 1893.

Confederate Veteran (Sumner A. Cunningham, ed.). 40 vols. Nashville, TN: Confederate Veteran, 1893-1932.

Cox, Jacob Dolson. *The March to the Sea: Franklin and Nashville*. New York, NY: Charles Scribner's Sons, 1882.

Davis, Jefferson. *The Rise and Fall of the Confederate Government*. 2 vols. New York, NY: D. Appleton and Co., 1881.

Dodd, Bella. *School of Darkness*. New York, NY: P. J. Kennedy and Sons, 1954.

Dodge, Grenville M. *The Battle of Atlanta and Other Campaigns, Addresses, Etc*. Council Bluffs, IA: self-published, 1910.

Evans, Clement Anselm (ed.). *Confederate Military History*. 12 vols. Atlanta, GA: Confederate Publishing Co., 1899.

Fiske, John. *The Mississippi Valley in the Civil War*. Cambridge, MA: Houghton, Mifflin and Co., 1902.

Franklin, John Hope. *Reconstruction After the Civil War*. Chicago, IL: University of Chicago Press, 1961.

Hasselberg, P. D. (ed.). *Parliamentary Debates: First Session, Fortieth Parliament, 1982, House of Representatives* (Vol. 445). Wellington, New Zealand: Government Printer, 1982.

Hood, John Bell. *Advance and Retreat: Personal Experiences in the United States and Confederate Armies*. New Orleans, LA: G. T. Beauregard, 1880.

Johnson, Richard W. *Memoir of Maj.-Gen. George H. Thomas*. Philadelphia, PA: J. B. Lippincott and Co., 1881.

Johnson, Robert Underwood, and Clarence Clough Buel (eds.). *Battles and Leaders of the Civil War*. 4 vols. New York, NY: The Century Co., 1884-1888.

Johnstone, Huger William. *Truth of War Conspiracy, 1861*. Idylwild, GA: H. W. Johnstone, 1921.

Jones, John William. *The Davis Memorial Volume; Or Our Dead President, Jefferson Davis and the World's Tribute to His Memory*. Richmond, VA: B. F. Johnson, 1889.

La Bree, Ben (ed.). *The Confederate Soldier in the Civil War, 1861-1865*. Louisville, KY: Prentice Press, 1897.

Lenin, Vladimir. *"Left Wing" Communism: An Infantile Disorder*. Detroit, MI: The Marxian Educational Society, 1921.

Livermore, Thomas L. *Numbers and Losses in the Civil War in America, 1861-65*. 1900. Carlisle, PA: John Kallmann, 1996 ed.

Magliocca, Gerard N. *The Tragedy of William Jennings Bryan: Constitutional Law and the Politics of Backlash*. New Haven, CT: Yale University Press, 2011.

Marx, Karl, and Frederick Engels. *Manifesto of the Communist Party*. Chicago, IL: Charles H. Kerr and Co., 1906.

McCarty, Burke (ed.). *Little Sermons in Socialism by Abraham Lincoln*. Chicago, IL: The Chicago Daily Socialist, 1910.

McMurray, William Josiah. *History of the Twentieth Tennessee Regiment Volunteer Infantry, C.S.A.* Nashville, TN: The Publication Committee, 1904.

McPherson, James M. *Abraham Lincoln and the Second American Revolution*. New York, NY: Oxford University Press, 1991.

Meriwether, Elizabeth Avery (pseudonym, "George Edmonds"). *Facts and Falsehoods Concerning the War on the South, 1861-1865*. Memphis, TN: A. R. Taylor and Co., 1904.

Miller, Francis Trevelyan, and Robert S. Lanier (eds.). *The Photographic History of the Civil War*. 10 vols. New York, NY: The Review of Reviews Co., 1911.

Minutes of the Eighth Annual Meeting and Reunion of the United Confederate Veterans, Atlanta, GA, July 20-23, 1898. New Orleans, LA: United Confederate Veterans, 1907.

Minutes of the Ninth Annual Meeting and Reunion of the United Confederate Veterans, Charleston, SC, May 10-13, 1899. New Orleans, LA: United Confederate Veterans, 1907.

Minutes of the Twelfth Annual Meeting and Reunion of the United Confederate Veterans, Dallas, TX, April 22-25, 1902. New Orleans, LA: United Confederate Veterans, 1907.

Muzzey, David Saville. *The United States of America: Vol. 1, To the Civil War*. Boston, MA: Ginn and Co., 1922.

——. *The American Adventure: Vol. 2, From the Civil War*. 1924. New York, NY: Harper and Brothers, 1927 ed.

Nicolay, John G., and John Hay (eds.). *Abraham Lincoln: A History*. 10 vols. New York, NY: The Century Co., 1890.

——. *Complete Works of Abraham Lincoln*. 12 vols. 1894. New York, NY: Francis D. Tandy Co., 1905 ed.

——. *Abraham Lincoln: Complete Works*. 12 vols. 1894. New York, NY: The Century Co., 1907 ed.

ORA (full title: *The War of the Rebellion: A Compilation of the Official Records of the Union and Confederate Armies*). 70 vols. Washington, DC: Government Printing Office, 1880.

ORN (full title: *Official Records of the Union and Confederate Navies in the War of the Rebellion*). 30 vols. Washington, DC: Government Printing Office, 1894.

Pollard, Edward Alfred. *The Lost Cause*. New York, NY: E. B. Treat and Co., 1867.

Richardson, John Anderson. *Richardson's Defense of the South*. Atlanta, GA: A. B. Caldwell, 1914.

Rogers, William P. *The Three Secession Movements in the United States: Samuel J. Tilden, the Democratic Candidate for Presidency; the Advisor, Aider and Abettor of the Great Secession Movement of 1860; and One of the Authors of the Infamous Resolution of 1864; His Claims as a Statesman and Reformer Considered*. Boston, MA: John Wilson and Son, 1876.

Rove, Karl. *The Triumph of William McKinley: Why the Election of 1896 Still Matters*. New York, NY: Simon and Schuster, 2015.

Rutherford, Mildred Lewis. *Truths of History: A Fair, Unbiased, Impartial, Unprejudiced and Conscientious Study of History*. Athens, GA: n.p., 1920.

Scofield, Levi T. *The Retreat From Pulaski to Nashville, Tenn.: Battle of Franklin, Tennessee, November 30th, 1864*. Cleveland, OH: Press of the Caxton Co., 1909.

Seabrook, Lochlainn. *Carnton Plantation Ghost Stories: True Tales of the Unexplained from Tennessee's Most Haunted Civil War House!* 2005. Franklin, TN, 2016 ed.

——. *Nathan Bedford Forrest: Southern Hero, American Patriot*. 2007. Franklin, TN, 2010 ed.

——. *Abraham Lincoln: The Southern View*. 2007. Franklin, TN: Sea Raven Press, 2013 ed.

——. *The McGavocks of Carnton Plantation: A Southern History - Celebrating One of Dixie's Most Noble Confederate Families and Their Tennessee Home*. 2008. Franklin, TN, 2011ed.

——. *A Rebel Born: A Defense of Nathan Bedford Forrest*. 2010. Franklin, TN: Sea Raven Press, 2011 ed.

——. *A Rebel Born: The Screenplay* (for the film). 2011. Franklin, TN: Sea Raven Press.

——. *Everything You Were Taught About the Civil War is Wrong, Ask a Southerner!* 2010. Franklin, TN: Sea Raven Press, revised 2014 ed.

——. *The Quotable Jefferson Davis: Selections From the Writings and Speeches of the Confederacy's First President*. Franklin, TN: Sea Raven Press, 2011.

——. *The Quotable Robert E. Lee: Selections From the Writings and Speeches of the South's Most Beloved Civil War General*. Franklin, TN: Sea Raven Press, 2011 Sesquicentennial Civil War Edition.

——. *Lincolnology: The Real Abraham Lincoln Revealed In His Own Words*. Franklin, TN: Sea Raven Press, 2011.

——. *The Unquotable Abraham Lincoln: The President's Quotes They Don't Want You To Know!* Franklin, TN: Sea Raven Press, 2011.

——. *Honest Jeff and Dishonest Abe: A Southern Children's Guide to the Civil War*. Franklin, TN: Sea Raven Press, 2012.

——. *Encyclopedia of the Battle of Franklin - A Comprehensive Guide to the Conflict that Changed the Civil War*. Franklin, TN: Sea Raven Press, 2012.

——. *The Quotable Nathan Bedford Forrest: Selections From the Writings and Speeches of the Confederacy's Most Brilliant Cavalryman*. Spring Hill, TN: Sea Raven Press, 2012.

——. *Forrest! 99 Reasons to Love Nathan Bedford Forrest*. Spring Hill, TN: Sea Raven Press, 2012.

——. *Give 'Em Hell Boys! The Complete Military Correspondence of Nathan Bedford Forrest*. Spring Hill, TN: Sea Raven Press, 2012.

——. *The Constitution of the Confederate States of America Explained: A Clause-by-Clause Study of the South's Magna Carta*. Spring Hill, TN: Sea Raven Press, 2012 Sesquicentennial Civil War Edition.

——. *The Great Impersonator: 99 Reasons to Dislike Abraham Lincoln*. Spring Hill, TN: Sea Raven Press, 2012.

——. *The Old Rebel: Robert E. Lee As He Was Seen By His Contemporaries*. Spring Hill, TN: Sea

Raven Press, 2012 Sesquicentennial Civil War Edition.

——. *The Quotable Stonewall Jackson: Selections From the Writings and Speeches of the South's Most Famous General*. Spring Hill, TN: Sea Raven Press, 2012 Sesquicentennial Civil War Edition.

——. *Saddle, Sword, and Gun: A Biography of Nathan Bedford Forrest for Teens*. Spring Hill, TN: Sea Raven Press, 2013.

——. *The Alexander H. Stephens Reader: Excerpts From the Works of a Confederate Founding Father*. Spring Hill, TN: Sea Raven Press, 2013.

——. *The Quotable Alexander H. Stephens: Selections From the Writings and Speeches of the Confederacy's First Vice President*. Spring Hill, TN: Sea Raven Press, 2013 Sesquicentennial Civil War Edition.

——. *Give This Book to a Yankee! A Southern Guide to the Civil War for Northerners*. Spring Hill, TN: Sea Raven Press, 2014.

——. *The Articles of Confederation Explained: A Clause-by-Clause Study of America's First Constitution*. Spring Hill, TN: Sea Raven Press, 2014.

——. *Confederate Blood and Treasure: An Interview With Lochlainn Seabrook*. Spring Hill, TN: Sea Raven Press, 2015.

——. *Nathan Bedford Forrest and the Battle of Fort Pillow: Yankee Myth, Confederate Fact*. Spring Hill, TN: Sea Raven Press, 2015.

——. *Everything You Were Taught About American Slavery War is Wrong, Ask a Southerner!* Spring Hill, TN: Sea Raven Press, 2015.

——. *Confederacy 101: Amazing Facts You Never Knew About America's Oldest Political Tradition*. Spring Hill, TN: Sea Raven Press, 2015.

——. *The Great Yankee Coverup: What the North Doesn't Want You to Know About Lincoln's War!* Spring Hill, TN: Sea Raven Press, 2015.

——. *Slavery 101: Amazing Facts You Never Knew About America's "Peculiar Institution."* Spring Hill, TN: Sea Raven Press, 2015.

——. *Confederate Flag Facts: What Every American Should Know About Dixie's Southern Cross*. Spring Hill, TN: Sea Raven Press, 2016.

——. *Nathan Bedford Forrest and the Ku Klux Klan: Yankee Myth, Confederate Fact*. Spring Hill, TN: Sea Raven Press, 2016.

——. *Seabrook's Bible Dictionary of Traditional and Mystical Christian Doctrines*. Spring Hill, TN: Sea Raven Press, 2016.

——. *Everything You Were Taught About African-Americans and the Civil War is Wrong, Ask a Southerner!* Spring Hill, TN: Sea Raven Press, 2016.

——. *Nathan Bedford Forrest and African-Americans: Yankee Myth, Confederate Fact*. Spring Hill, TN: Sea Raven Press, 2016.

——. *Women in Gray: A Tribute to the Ladies Who Supported the Southern Confederacy*. Spring Hill, TN: Sea Raven Press, 2016.

——. *Lincoln's War: The Real Cause, the Real Winner, the Real Loser*. Spring Hill, TN: Sea Raven Press, 2016.

——. *The Unholy Crusade: Lincoln's Legacy of Destruction in the American South*. Spring Hill, TN: Sea Raven Press, 2017.

——. *Abraham Lincoln Was a Liberal, Jefferson Davis Was a Conservative: The Missing Key to Understanding the American Civil War*. Spring Hill, TN: Sea Raven Press, 2017.

——. *All We Ask is to be Let Alone: The Southern Secession Fact Book*. Spring Hill, TN: Sea Raven Press, 2017.

——. *The Ultimate Civil War Quiz Book: How Much Do You Really Know About America's Most Misunderstood Conflict?* Spring Hill, TN: Sea Raven Press, 2017.

——. *Rise Up and Call Them Blessed: Victorian Tributes to the Confederate Soldier, 1861-1901*. Spring Hill, TN: Sea Raven Press, 2017.

——. *Victorian Confederate Poetry: The Southern Cause in Verse, 1861-1901.* Spring Hill, TN: Sea Raven Press, 2018.

——. *Confederate Monuments: Why Every American Should Honor Confederate Soldiers and Their Memorials.* Spring Hill, TN: Sea Raven Press, 2018.

——. *The God of War: Nathan Bedford Forrest as He Was Seen by His Contemporaries.* Spring Hill, TN: Sea Raven Press, 2018.

——. *The Battle of Spring Hill: Recollections of Confederate and Union Soldiers.* Spring Hill, TN: Sea Raven Press, 2018.

——. *I Rode With Forrest! Confederate Soldiers Who Served With the World's Greatest Cavalry Leader.* Spring Hill, TN: Sea Raven Press, 2018.

——. *The Battle of Franklin: Recollections of Confederate and Union Soldiers.* Spring Hill, TN: Sea Raven Press, 2018.

Steel, Samuel Augustus. *The South Was Right.* Columbia, SC: R. L. Bryan Co., 1914.

Stephens, Alexander Hamilton. *Speech of Mr. Stephens, of Georgia, on the War and Taxation.* Washington, D.C.: J & G. Gideon, 1848.

——. *A Constitutional View of the Late War Between the States; Its Causes, Character, Conduct and Results.* 2 vols. Philadelphia, PA: National Publishing, Co., 1870.

——. *Recollections of Alexander H. Stephens: His Diary Kept When a Prisoner at Fort Warren, Boston Harbour, 1865.* New York, NY: Doubleday, Page, and Co., 1910.

Thompson, Holland. *The New South: A Chronicle of Social and Industrial Evolution.* New Haven, CT: Yale University Press, 1920.

Van Horne, Thomas B. *History of the Army of the Cumberland: Its Organization, Campaigns, and Battles.* 2 vols. Cincinnati, OH: Robert Clarke and Co., 1875.

Warner, Ezra J. *Generals in Gray: Lives of the Confederate Commanders.* 1959. Baton Rouge, LA: Louisiana State University Press, 1989 ed.

——. *Generals in Blue: Lives of the Union Commanders.* 1964. Baton Rouge, LA: Louisiana State University Press, 2006 ed.

Wilson, John Laird. *The Pictorial History of the Great Civil War: Its Causes, Origin, Conduct and Results.* Philadelphia, PA: The National Publishing Co., 1878.

Woods, Thomas E., Jr. *The Politically Incorrect Guide to American History.* Washington, D.C.: Regnery, 2004.

Wooldrige, John (ed.). *History of Nashville, Tenn.* Nashville, TN: H. W. Crew, 1890.

Another view of the Yankee outer lines, Nashville, Tenn., the final day of the battle, December 16, 1864.

MEET THE AUTHOR

LOCHLAINN SEABROOK, a neo-Victorian and world acclaimed man of letters, is a Kentucky Colonel and the winner of the prestigious Jefferson Davis Historical Gold Medal for his "masterpiece," *A Rebel Born: A Defense of Nathan Bedford Forrest*. A classic littérateur and an unreconstructed Southern historian, he is an award-winning author, "Civil War" scholar, Confederate culture expert, Bible authority, the leading popularizer of American Civil War history, and a traditional Southern Agrarian of Scottish, English, Irish, Dutch, Welsh, German, and Italian extraction.

A child prodigy of Revolutionary, Southern, and Confederate blood, Seabrook is today a true Renaissance Man whose occupational titles also include encyclopedist, lexicographer, musician, artist, graphic designer, genealogist, photographer, and award-winning poet. Also a songwriter and a screenwriter, he has a 40 year background in historical nonfiction writing and is a member of the Sons of Confederate Veterans, the Civil War Trust, and the National Grange.

Known to his many fans as the "voice of the traditional South," due to similarities in their writing styles, ideas, and literary works, Seabrook is also often referred to as the "new Shelby Foote," the "Southern Joseph Campbell," and the "American Robert Graves" (his English cousin). Seabrook coined the terms "South-shaming" and "Lincolnian liberalism," and holds the world's record for writing the most books on Nathan Bedford Forrest. In addition, Seabrook is the first Civil War scholar to connect the early American nickname for the U.S., "The Confederate States of America," with the Southern Confederacy that arose eight decades later, and the first to note that in 1860 the party platforms of the two major political parties were the opposite of what they are today (Victorian Democrats were Conservatives, Victorian Republicans were Liberals).

Above, Colonel Lochlainn Seabrook, "the voice of the traditional South," award-winning Civil War scholar and unreconstructed Southern historian. America's most popular and prolific pro-South author, his many books have introduced hundreds of thousands to the truth about the War for Southern Independence. He coined the phrase "South-shaming" and holds the world record for writing the most books on Nathan Bedford Forrest.

The son of a Kentucky trainman and the grandson of Appalachian coal-mining and farming families, Seabrook is a seventh-generation Kentuckian whose European ancestors came from Virginia, North Carolina, and Tennessee, settling in the Bluegrass State in the early 1700s, thereafter spreading into West Virginia, the Midwest, and finally the West. He has over a dozen ancestors who fought in the American Revolutionary War, including such family surnames as Bentley, Combs, Mullins, Crase/Kress, Adkins, Kelly, Nelson, Shannon, McBrayer, Hutchinson, and Leslie.

Seabrook is co-chair of the Jent/Gent Family Committee (Kentucky), founder and director of the Blakeney Family Tree Project, and a board member of the Friends of Colonel Benjamin E. Caudill. His literary works have been endorsed by leading authorities, museum curators, award-winning historians, bestselling authors, celebrities, filmmakers, noted scientists, well regarded educators, TV show hosts and producers, renowned military artists, esteemed Southern organizations, and distinguished academicians from around the world.

Seabrook has authored over 60 popular adult books on the American Civil War, American and international slavery, the U.S. Confederacy (1781), the Southern Confederacy (1861), religion, theology, thealogy, Jesus, the Bible, the Apocrypha, the Law of Attraction, alternative health, spirituality, ghost stories, the paranormal, ufology, social issues, and cross-cultural studies of the family and marriage. His Confederate biographies, pro-South studies, Victorian Southern literature titles, genealogical monographs, family histories, biographical and military encyclopedias, self-help guides, and etymological dictionaries have received wide acclaim.

Seabrook's eight children's books include a Southern guide to the "Civil War," a biography of Nathan Bedford Forrest, a dictionary of religion and myth, a rewriting of the King Arthur legend (which reinstates the original pre-Christian motifs), two bedtime stories for preschoolers, a naturalist's guidebook to owls, a worldwide look at the family, and an examination of the Near-Death Experience.

Of blue-blooded Southern stock through his Kentucky, Tennessee, Virginia, North Carolina and West Virginia ancestors, he is a direct descendant of European royalty via his 6th great-grandfather, the Earl of Oxford, after which London's famous Harley Street is named. Among his celebrated male Celtic ancestors is Robert the Bruce, King of Scotland, Seabrook's 22nd great-grandfather. The 21st great-grandson of Edward I "Longshanks" Plantagenet), King of England, Seabrook is a 17th-generation Southerner through his descent from the colonists of Jamestown, Virginia (1607).

The 2nd, 3rd, and 4th great-grandson of dozens of Confederate soldiers, one of his closest connections to Lincoln's War is through his 3rd great-grandfather, Elias Jent Sr., who fought for the Confederacy in the Thirteenth Cavalry Kentucky under Seabrook's 2nd cousin, Colonel Benjamin E. Caudill. The Thirteenth,

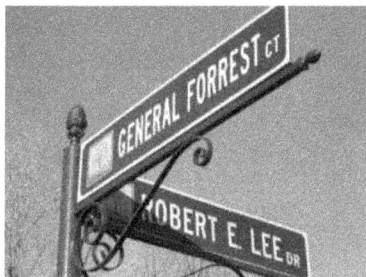

(Photo © Lochlainn Seabrook)

also known as "Caudill's Army," fought in numerous conflicts, including the Battles of Saltville, Gladsville, Mill Cliff, Poor Fork, Whitesburg, and Leatherwood.

Seabrook is a direct descendant of the families of Alexander H. Stephens, John Singleton Mosby, William Giles Harding, and Edmund Winchester Rucker, and is related to the following Confederates and other 18th- and 19th-Century luminaries: Robert E. Lee, Stephen Dill Lee, Stonewall Jackson, Nathan Bedford Forrest, James Longstreet, John Hunt Morgan, Jeb Stuart, Pierre G. T. Beauregard (approved the Confederate Battle Flag design), George W. Gordon, John Bell Hood, Alexander Peter Stewart, Arthur M. Manigault, Joseph Manigault, Charles Scott Venable, Thornton A. Washington, John A. Washington, Abraham Buford, Edmund W. Pettus, Theodrick "Tod" Carter, John B. Womack, John H. Winder, Gideon J. Pillow, States Rights Gist, Henry R. Jackson, John Lawton Seabrook, John C. Breckinridge, Leonidas Polk, Zachary Taylor, Sarah Knox Taylor (first wife of Jefferson Davis), Richard Taylor, Davy Crockett, Daniel Boone, Meriwether Lewis (of the Lewis and Clark Expedition) Andrew Jackson, James K. Polk, Abram Poindexter Maury (founder of Franklin, TN), Zebulon Baird Vance, Thomas

Jefferson, Edmund Jennings Randolph, George Wythe Randolph (grandson of Jefferson), Felix K. Zollicoffer, Fitzhugh Lee, Nathaniel F. Cheairs, Jesse James, Frank James, Robert Brank Vance, Charles Sidney Winder, John W. McGavock, Caroline E. (Winder) McGavock, David Harding McGavock, Lysander McGavock, James Randal McGavock, Randal William McGavock, Francis McGavock, Emily McGavock, William Henry F. Lee, Lucius E. Polk, Minor Meriwether (husband of noted pro-South author Elizabeth Avery Meriwether), Ellen Bourne Tynes (wife of Forrest's chief of artillery, Captain John W. Morton), South Carolina Senators Preston Smith Brooks and Andrew Pickens Butler, and famed South Carolina diarist Mary Chesnut.

Seabrook's modern day cousins include: Patrick J. Buchanan (conservative author), Cindy Crawford (model), Shelby Lee Adams (Letcher Co., Kentucky, photographer), Bertram Thomas Combs (Kentucky's 50th governor), Edith Bolling (second wife of President Woodrow Wilson), and actors Andy Griffith, Riley Keough, George C. Scott, Robert Duvall, Reese Witherspoon, Lee Marvin, Rebecca Gayheart, and Tom Cruise.

Seabrook's screenplay, *A Rebel Born*, based on his book of the same name, has been signed with acclaimed filmmaker Christopher Forbes (of Forbes Film). Set for release as a full-length feature film, it is in pre-production, awaiting the necessary funding. This will be the first movie ever made of Nathan Bedford Forrest's life story, and as a historically accurate project written from the Southern perspective, is destined to be one of the most talked about Civil War films of all time.

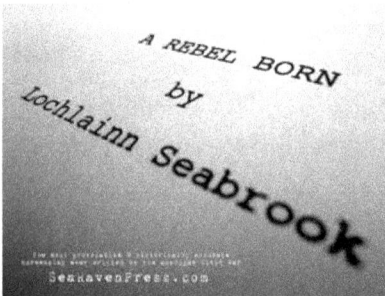

Born with music in his blood, Seabrook is an award-winning, multi-genre, BMI-Nashville songwriter and lyricist who has composed some 3,000 songs (250 albums), and whose original music has been heard in film (*A Rebel Born, Cowgirls 'n Angels, Confederate Cavalry, Billy the Kid: Showdown in Lincoln County, Vengeance Without Mercy, Last Step, County Line, The Mark*) and on TV and radio worldwide. A musician, producer, multi-instrumentalist, and renown performer—whose keyboard work has been variously compared to pianists from Hargus Robbins and Vince Guaraldi to Elton John and Leonard Bernstein—Seabrook has opened for groups such as the Earl Scruggs Review, Ted Nugent, and Bob Seger, and has performed privately for such public figures as President Ronald Reagan, Burt Reynolds, Loni Anderson, and Senator Edward W. Brooke. Seabrook's cousins in the music business include: Johnny Cash, Elvis Presley, Lisa Marie Presley, Billy Ray and Miley Cyrus, Patty Loveless, Tim McGraw, Lee Ann Womack, Dolly Parton, Pat Boone, Naomi, Wynonna, and Ashley Judd, Ricky Skaggs, the Sunshine Sisters, Martha Carson, and Chet Atkins.

Seabrook lives with his wife and family in historic Middle Tennessee, the heart of Forrest country and the Confederacy, where his conservative Southern ancestors fought valiantly against Liberal Lincoln and the progressive North in defense of Jeffersonianism, constitutional government, and personal liberty.

For more info visit

LOCHLAINNSEABROOK.COM

If you enjoyed this book you will be interested in Colonel Seabrook's other popular related titles:

☞ ABRAHAM LINCOLN WAS A LIBERAL, JEFFERSON DAVIS WAS A CONSERVATIVE
☞ EVERYTHING YOU WERE TAUGHT ABOUT THE CIVIL WAR IS WRONG, ASK A SOUTHERNER!
☞ ALL WE ASK IS TO BE LET ALONE: THE SOUTHERN SECESSION FACT BOOK
☞ EVERYTHING YOU WERE TAUGHT ABOUT AMERICAN SLAVERY IS WRONG, ASK A SOUTHERNER!
☞ CONFEDERATE FLAG FACTS: WHAT EVERY AMERICAN SHOULD KNOW ABOUT DIXIE'S SOUTHERN CROSS
☞ LINCOLN'S WAR: THE REAL CAUSE, THE REAL WINNER, THE REAL LOSER

Available from Sea Raven Press and wherever fine books are sold

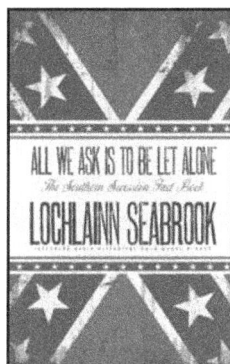

SeaRavenPress.com • NathanBedfordForrestBooks.com